HOW TO BE A BETTER RIDER

THE ESSENTIAL GUIDE

"We make a conscious decision to ride and enjoy the thrill and freedom that life on two wheels delivers."

A testimonial from the authors

For most of us motorcycling is a passion. While the majority of drivers use a car out of necessity, we make a conscious decision to ride motorcycles and enjoy the thrill and freedom that life on two wheels delivers.

Even those who come to motorcycling for purely practical reasons soon discover the fun to be had. After that there's no turning back. Which is probably why increasing numbers of riders are appreciating the benefits of post-test training, because as your riding improves, so does your level of enjoyment.

With that in mind, we hope you will find this book useful. Its aim is to introduce you to the key mental and physical skills that will help you to become a better rider, whilst enabling you to pass the Institute of Advanced Motorists' advanced motorcycling test.

We won't pretend that you will be able to learn and apply all the principles in this book overnight. It will take time. As your skills improve you will become a safer more progressive rider, getting even more fun out of your motorcycling. Good luck and safe riding!

Stefan Bartlett - Head of Motorcycle Publishing, Bauer Media
Jon Taylor - IAM Staff Examiner

© 2009 the Institute of Advanced Motorists. Published by the Institute of Advanced Motorists, IAM House, 510 Chiswick High Rd, London W4 5RG.

FIRST EDITION
All rights reserved. No part of this publication may be reproduced or transmitted in any form or by any means, electronic or mechanical, including photocopying, recording or in any information storage retrieval system, without the prior written permission of the IAM.

Words by Stefan Bartlett
Advanced riding consultation by Jon Taylor
Photographs by Adam Duckworth
Design by Mark Guest
Reprographics by AT Graphics
Printed by Think Publishing in the UK
ISBN 978-0-9562239-1-3

HOW TO BE A BETTER RIDER
THE ESSENTIAL GUIDE

Experience the pleasure of riding safely and progressively

HOW TO USE THIS BOOK

This book should be used for self-study and to supplement expert advice from the Institute of Advanced Motorists' representatives in preparation for taking the Advanced Riding Test. The way it is organised allows you to find the relevant subjects and advice quickly and easily under general headings. The most important aspects of Advanced Riding are summarised at the end of each of the major topics, under the headings:

Rider checklist – *What you should be achieving.*
Examiner checklist – *What the examiner is looking for you to achieve.*

How to be a better rider - the essential guide

CONTENTS

1 PREPARING TO RIDE

2 BASIC PRINCIPLES OF ADVANCED RIDING

3 RIDING TECHNIQUES IN ACTION

IAM contact details
www.iam.org.uk

What advanced riding is about

- Being in total control... all the time
- Understanding what you are doing
- Quick, efficient and safe overtaking
- Anticipating other road-users' mistakes
- Progressive riding where conditions allow
- Becoming a thinking rider, not an automaton
- Understanding your motorcycle, and getting the most out of it
- Developing observation, anticipation and timing at junctions and roundabouts, so you can negotiate the traffic with minimal disruption

GO ON, GET INVOLVED

By reading this book and showing an interest in advanced riding, you're already well on the way to improving your riding skills, making you far less likely to be involved in an accident. Advanced riding isn't for everyone, but by studying this book and applying what you learn, you WILL become a better rider. You'll learn to ride with greater precision and awareness, anticipate the danger created by other road users' mistakes and allow a big enough safety margin to avoid getting into trouble. You don't need to ride slowly, always worrying about what danger might be around the next bend in order to be safe. Instead, think ahead, so you're confident, decisive, and always able to make good progress.

HOW YOU'LL BENEFIT FROM TAKING THE ADVANCED RIDING TEST

This book will help you prepare to take the advanced riding challenge, which in turn will give you the confidence of knowing you're a safe, more competent and more courteous rider. When you pass, you'll become part of an ever-growing band of advanced riders and enjoy all the benefits that brings. You'll be far less likely to crash your machine than you would have been before your training. Many insurance companies give substantial discounts to advanced riders, so your test fees could easily be repaid in the first years after you pass. You also get many other benefits of being an IAM member and gain a valuable skill for life.

HOW TO BECOME AN IAM ADVANCED RIDER

This book contains all the information you need to become a better rider – an IAM advanced rider. Combine the contents of this book with a little commitment, and expert help from the IAM's trained volunteer observers, and you could be experiencing all the benefits of being a qualified advanced rider in a matter of months. Read this book, learn and practise all the key points, then sign up for the Skill For Life riding course.

SIGNING UP TO *SKILL FOR LIFE*

Skill For life can be taken in two ways:
The standard Skill For Life course is run by the IAM's volunteer force of trained observers. You take as long as you need to prepare for the test – a typical rider takes about eight sessions to prepare for the 90-minute test. Skill For Life can be completed more quickly through IAM Fleet Training with the help of a professional trainer. This involves a one-day or two half-day intensive sessions with one trainee to one professional coach, followed, once you're ready, by the 90-minute test. At the conclusion of your formal training or observed rides, your test application will be submitted by your trainer or observer. You will then be contacted by an examiner in your area to arrange the test.

Taking the IAM advanced riding test

- You'll meet up with the examiner at an agreed location. There are over 300 IAM examiners around the UK.

- You take the test on your own motorcycle, which must be road legal.

- A valid driving licence, insurance policy and MOT certificate (if required) must be presented before the test can begin.

- The test takes about 90 minutes and covers 35 to 40 miles.

- The route will incorporate all types of roads and conditions: Motorways (where possible), dual carriageways, country roads and urban streets.

- You should ride the way you have been shown by your fleet trainer or volunteer observer.

- You must always stick to the speed limits, whilst riding as progressively as conditions allow.

- You may be asked to demonstrate some simple, slow-speed manoeuvring skills.

- At the end, the examiner – who will be a trained police motorcycle rider and police advanced car driver – will tell you whether you will be recommended for full membership. If you are not recommended you can retake the test at a later date.

- The test is presented in a friendly, non-intimidating way.

- A few minor faults don't preclude you from becoming a full IAM member, but infringements of the law will not be condoned.

It's a jungle out

Each time you ride your motorcycle on the road, you face a
Check out this picture. It highlights the sort of risks you could

OTHER BIKERS
Never rise to
the challenge
from other
motorcyclists to race.

**WORN/UNEVEN
ROAD SURFACE**
Potholes and
'tramlines' left by
HGVs present a unique
danger to motorcyclists

there!

whole host of potential dangers.
face in your everyday riding

UNFIT DRIVERS
Drivers with poor eyesight, untested drivers and drivers on medication all present a lethal risk to motorcyclists

DIESEL SPILLAGES
Grip is everything on a motorcycle. Diesel spillages reduce it to zero. Beware!

TIRED DRIVERS
After extended periods behind the wheel, the average motorist loses awareness and accuracy

OTHER HAZARDS
- unsignalled manoeuvres
- car with broken brake lights
- wet road markings
- bad visibility
- strong winds
- low, blinding sunlight
- over banding (see page 32)

These are just a few of the hazards you'll discover on Britain's roads. The IAM's *Skill For Life* test prepares you to deal with all of them.

The standard riding test

The standard L-test only involves learning the most fundamental riding skills. The more you develop your riding abilities, the greater the enjoyment you will get from your machine

The Government has made the standard L-test more difficult in recent years, with the addition of a two-part test, graded machine entitlements, multiple-choice written test and a computerised hazard-awareness assessment. However, it still only involves learning the most fundamental riding skills and doesn't include preparation for poor weather or motorway riding. It is only an introduction to motorcycle riding. This is where IAM advanced rider education comes in. The more in-depth and rounded content of Skill For Life will prepare you for

virtually any situation you're likely to encounter – and give you the observation skills and anticipation to avoid many incidents and hazards you were previously unaware of. It will take your riding significantly beyond the 'L' test and the DSA Enhanced-Rider Scheme. That said, even experienced advanced riders continue to learn and hone their skills every time they get on their machine. Banishing all the bad habits you've developed since passing your test is another good reason to become an advanced rider. Simply applying what you learn in this book will make

"The more in-depth content of Skill For Life will prepare you for virtually any situation."

every journey safer, smoother and at the same time, quicker and more enjoyable.
The better you become as a rider, the more fun you get from your machine.

Your safety depends on the condition of your motorcycle. Clean your lights, number-plate and mirrors regularly, and spend just 10 minutes a week checking your machine's fluid levels, lights, tyre pressures and tread depth. This will improve your safety and also get the best performance, economy and reliability from your machine.

Your state of mind

On the UK's congested roads it's important that you're always in the right frame of mind to ride. Positive attitudes will help to reduce the risk of collisions through tolerance and courtesy, by being realistic as to your own abilities, and by maintaining a high degree of care for your own safety and that of others.

Riding on UK roads can be stressful, so always aim to remain cool-headed, tolerant and courteous – helping to avoid or diffuse any threatening situations. Don't let your riding standards be affected by other drivers' mistakes or behaviour. Don't be provoked and remember that, if you do make a mistake, an apologetic wave is often all it takes to put things right.

Avoid riding if you..

● Are feeling fatigued. (You should not ride for more than two hours at a time without a break.)
● Have flu.
● Are stressed or feel aggressive after, say, a bad day at work or a row at home.
● Have consumed alcohol.
● Have taken any drugs – even some mild medicines such as a cold treatments, may make you feel drowsy.

Don't let your enthusiasm for riding tempt you into breaking the speed limit or riding dangerously. Avoid riding in this way, always know what speed you are doing and what the maximum speed limit is. Likewise timid riders can be just as dangerous as aggressive ones. Aim to ride decisively and always display a high level of self-control, having planned your next manoeuvre.

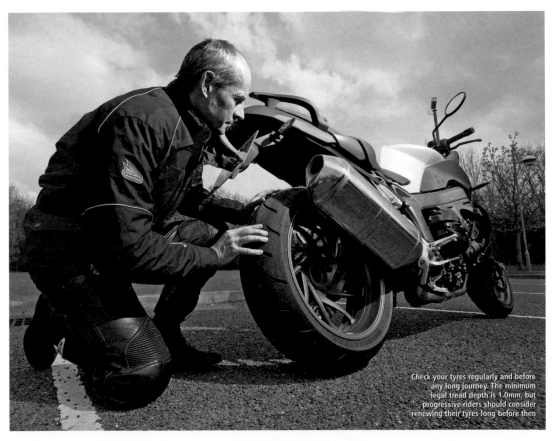

Check your tyres regularly and before any long journey. The minimum legal tread depth is 1.0mm, but progressive riders should consider renewing their tyres long before then

How to be a better rider

ALWAYS ROOM FOR IMPROVEMENT

Whether you're a novice rider or an experienced motorcyclist, you'll find there's always room to improve your riding skills. Keep an open mind, be realistic about your limitations and always be prepared to learn from any errors you make.

Experienced advanced riders learn from any mistakes they make

YOUR REACTION TIME

Your thinking distance varies with the speed of the machine, your physical and mental condition and the degree of concentration applied. Even with lightning reflexes and at legal speeds, the distance your machine covers before you can get your hand/foot onto the brake lever/pedal in an emergency is considerable. And that doesn't take into account the braking distance itself. Your reactions slow when you are tired, cold, ill or stressed. Drugs and drink also have a negative effect, but may actually make you think you're reacting more quickly than normal.

If you suspect imminent danger ahead, position your hand and foot over the brakes. This will save valuable milliseconds if the worst happens, but take care not to ride like that as a matter of course. The graph below shows the distances it takes to react (not brake) at various speeds. It assumes an unrealistically fast reaction time of just 0.65 seconds – this is a best case scenario. Most, if not all, riders would take longer than this to react to a hazard in a real life situation. Your aim when riding should always be to give yourself plenty of time to react.

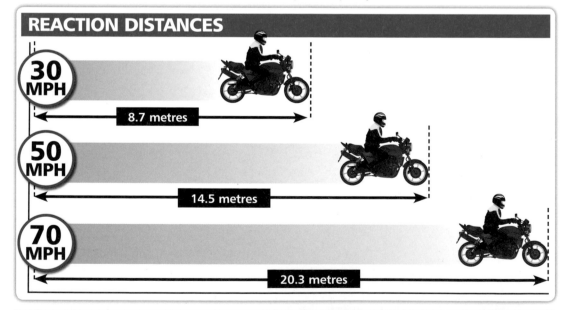

REACTION DISTANCES

30 MPH — 8.7 metres

50 MPH — 14.5 metres

70 MPH — 20.3 metres

OTHER PEOPLE'S REACTIONS

Always expect the worst from other road users. If you allow for poor observation and slow reactions, you'll find you're always prepared for the worst-case scenario.

When following other vehicles, (unless you're about to pass) always apply the two-second rule (see page 42). If you suspect they may not be totally focused on their driving, leave an even bigger gap to give yourself extra braking time. Tailgating is a common cause of collisions, it is dangerous and antisocial and can never be condoned.

Clothing

An important part of riding is wearing the right kit to keep you warm, dry and safe. Any clothing needs to be a compromise between comfort and protection.

Specialist motorcycle clothing stores offer a wide range of kit and expert advice. Look for CE approval on all equipment for guaranteed levels of protection. Bear in mind that the actual fit of the clothing is an essential part of its ability to protect the rider.

Visibility.

A very common excuse made by drivers who have pulled out in front of a motorcyclist, is that they didn't see them. High-visibility jackets (including hi-vis arms) are the clothing most easily seen by motorists, especially in poor weather. By following the advice in the *Highway Code,* you'll minimise the risk of an accident and ensure that any compensation awarded in these circumstances isn't reduced.

Helmets

When buying a crash helmet, visit a specialist shop where you'll get expert help and advice and a helmet that fits perfectly. Helmets don't last forever. Many factors affect the lifespan of a helmet, and you should think about changing your helmet every three to five years.

If you drop your helmet on a hard surface from more than, say, a metre, it should be replaced even if there is no visible damage.

Always ensure the visor system operates smoothly and that the visor is legal. Never use a tinted visor at night.

Gloves

These should be light and flexible enough to allow accurate 'feel' for the controls, whilst at the same time being strong enough to give sufficient protection. In winter, thicker gloves may be necessary to withstand the colder temperatures. A good compromise can sometimes be had by using thinner gloves with either heated elements inside or with heated handlebar grips to give the best of both worlds.

Jackets & Trousers

Motorcycle clothing made from modern man-made materials is now arguably easier to live with than traditional leathers. Go for a jacket that is both waterproof and windproof, with a detachable thermal lining.

The level of protection offered by a quality set of leathers is difficult to beat though. On track days, one-piece or two-piece zip-together leathers may be compulsory.

Boots

Ensure that any boots you wear fully cover the vulnerable ankle area and offer a suitable level of protection. Many modern boots have a waterproof membrane that allows the comfort, fit and protection of a good quality leather boot, but the water-proofing of a synthetic one.

GORE-TEX®
Performance Shell

Riding position

Achieving the best riding position is essential for the advanced motorcyclist. The correct position allows excellent control over your machine, maximum comfort and enhanced alertness, even on long journeys.

To check your riding position, put your bike on the centre stand (or get someone to support it from the rear). Sit on the seat in your normal riding gear and lightly grip the handlebars. How does this feel?

Ask the following questions:
● Does your clothing let you operate the controls effectively?
● Can you easily move your feet so that the ball of your foot rests on the footpeg?
● Do you have enough leg movement to avoid cutting off the blood supply to your lower limbs on a long ride?
● Can you look well ahead to the horizon without your helmet or clothing applying pressure to the back of your neck?
● Are your arms slightly bent at the elbows?
● When resting your fingers lightly above the controls, do they make a straight line from your elbow to your finger tips in your normal riding position?
● Is the span of your fingers

sufficient to allow you good control at the engagement point of both levers?
● Can you work the rear-brake/ gear levers without swivelling your foot unnecessarily?

Remember, you may be riding for long periods. If you are uncomfortable or your control is compromised, this affects your concentration levels and ultimately your safety.

Make sure you know all the controls on your machine, such as the horn, light switches, indicators, headlight flash and engine cut-off.

If in doubt check the manufacturer's handbook.

Forearm position
Ideally, your elbows should be slightly below your wrists. The closer to 90-degrees the angle of your forearms are to that of the fork legs, the more efficient your steering inputs will become.

Foot location
For normal riding, keeping the balls of your feet on the footrest avoids scraping them on the ground when cornering, or them being trapped beneath the machine in the event of a spill.

Elbow position

Try standing in front of a door or wall. Hold your fists in front of you, shoulder width apart, as if holding a handlebar, with your elbows stuck out. Now try pushing against the door or wall.

Now bring your elbows in to your sides and try it again. See the difference? You also get to see your mirrors clearly!

Lever Position

Adjust your levers so that, when resting your fingers on top of them, it makes a straight line back to your elbows.

STARTING THE ENGINE

Take the time to read your motorcycle's handbook and ensure you are familiar with how your machine operates.
● Take the machine off its stand and sit astride it.
● Ensure that the motorcycle is in neutral by gently rocking it backwards and forwards.
● Cover the rear brake and turn on the ignition.
● Check the neutral indicator is lit (if you have one fitted).
● Pull in the clutch lever.

● Start the engine.
● Make sure all the appropriate warning lights go out and ensure you know what they refer to, e.g: ABS, oil pressure and fuel level. Check the manual if any lights stay on.

Do you know what all these lights and controls are for?

MIRRORS

Check your mirrors before every journey.
- Ensure they are clean and clear.
- Position them to achieve the best view both behind you and to the sides. (The use of blind-spot mirrors, positioned where your vision might otherwise be obscured by handlebars or elbows, can help greatly).
- Ensure that you are aware of any blind spots (see below).

Clean mirrors guarantee excellent rear visibility

The 'blind-spot check' over your shoulder is an essential part of advanced riding

HOW TO CHECK FOR BLIND SPOTS

Ask someone to slowly walk behind you from side to side and note the points at which they disappear from view, then reappear. These are your blind spots and on some motorcycles, particularly on wide roads, they can be big enough to hide an entire lorry! Be aware of these zones and compensate by making more frequent checks if necessary.

Once underway, glance regularly in your mirrors to note the relative position of other vehicles as they approach from the rear, and note how that position changes. If necessary, stop and re-adjust your mirrors to minimise the blind-spot delay. When doing this, ensure you are in the correct riding position.

Before any manoeuvre you make, consider taking a quick look over your shoulder to check that you haven't missed anything in the blind spot. (See 'Blind Spot Check' on page 31)

Ensure that you are in the correct riding position before adjusting your mirrors

IF CARRYING A PILLION PASSENGER

- Will their seating position compromise your control of your machine or view behind?
- Do they have the correct clothing/equipment?
- Are they provided with footrests that they can comfortably reach?
- Have they ridden on the back of a motorcycle before – if not, some advice as to what they can expect from you and what you will expect from them, will prove useful.

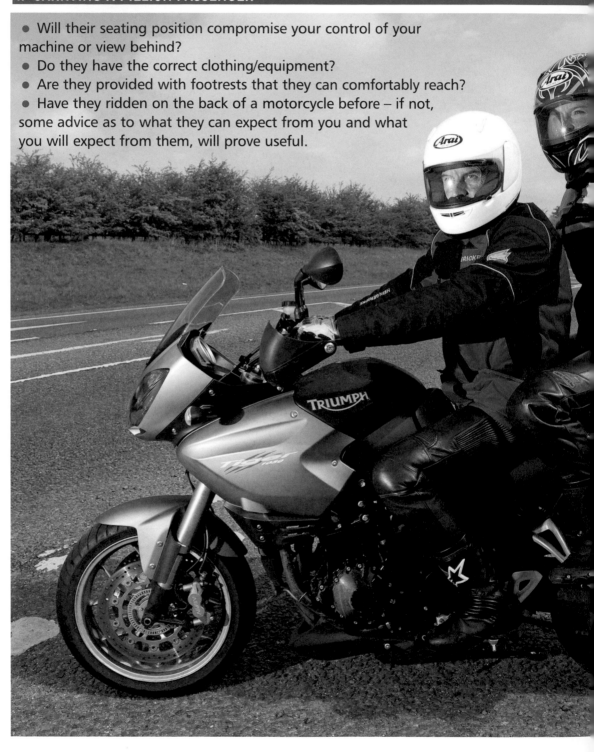

ON-BIKE RIDING AIDS

Satellite navigation

Sat nav systems are becoming increasingly popular. If you have one, program it before setting off on your trip. Save time by adding all relevant destinations to the unit's memory. Where possible, position the screen close to your eye-line (but not obstructing your view) so that you can see it easily without taking your eyes too far off the road. Always plan a route in advance and DO NOT rely on satellite navigation as your sole source of information. Occasionally, one-way systems, fords or unclassified roads, for example, may not be accurately represented.

"Position your sat nav as close to your eye-line as possible, without obstructing your view."

RIDER CHECKLIST
- Maintain your machine regularly and keep it road legal.
- Ensure all controls are positioned correctly.
- Keep the mirrors clean and correctly adjusted.
- Familiarise yourself with all the controls of the machine by reading the manufacturer's handbook.
- Keep your visor clear.

EXAMINER CHECKLIST
- Is the motorcycle well-maintained, in a roadworthy condition and road legal?
- Is the rider familiar with the machine controls and are they adjusted correctly?
- Is the riding position correct?
- Are all mirrors adjusted properly?
- Is the rider appropriately dressed for the conditions?

2 // BASIC PRINCIPLES OF ADVANCED RIDING

Hazards

The UK's busy roads are full of potential dangers. Learn to spot these hazards early and take appropriate action

A hazard is anything that contains an element of actual or potential danger

A hazard is anything that contains an element of actual or potential danger. That includes junctions, roundabouts, hillcrests and bends as well as the position and movement of other road users and even the weather. Imagine combining several of these elements in one scenario and you have a massive potential for danger. A roundabout, traffic lights or right turn, are all hazards – not just a child running into the street, a blind bend or an accident black spot. This means that it is essential for you to position your machine correctly when dealing with them, giving you that one essential ingredient – sufficient time to react.

Imagine almost any accident situation, if you had sufficient warning you would almost certainly be able to avoid it. This is the cornerstone of a planned system of riding.

> ⚠ Recognising the 'Limit Point' of your vision (see page 68), and learning observational techniques to extend it, lets you plan ahead much more effectively.

WHY YOU NEED TO THINK AHEAD

On pages 12 and 13 we showed you just some of the potential dangers you could face every time you ride your machine. To minimise your chances of being affected by adverse riding conditions, or other people's mistakes, you need to take a planned and systematic approach to your riding. This means you'll anticipate hazards, spot them earlier and allow enough time and space to avoid them all together. Even in the worst-case scenario, you'll give yourself enough time to take effective evasive action.

Thinking ahead means that every manoeuvre is made in good time and under control.

So many hazards, so little time! But which way does the road go?

Probably not the way you were expecting!

In busy urban scenarios hazards are everywhere

Don't focus on one major hazard too intently. You may miss others

Is this rider in the correct position for all three hazards (see dots)?

A planned system

A GOOD INSTINCT TO HAVE

Approaching your riding in a systematic way, quickly helps you to improve your motorcycling skills. It is especially beneficial in difficult riding situations, as it lets you manage hazards in a calm, planned, efficient and flexible manner.

The early recognition of hazards such as physical features, the position and movement of other road users, the changes in road surface and the weather, gives you time to plan your progress.

TIME TO REACT

Physical features include junctions, roundabouts, bends and hillcrests. Generally, they're simple to deal with systematically, but can be complicated by their layout and the movements of other road-users. If you then add a diesel spillage, ice, or heavy rain into the equation, you have a much more hazardous situation, and one that requires the use of a planned riding system to give you time to assess and react to all potential dangers. The IAM's Skill For Life course incorporates an excellent five-part riding system, which you can apply to every riding manoeuvre you make. It's called IPSGA.

I

INFORMATION
Absorb Information: Always observe everything around you, including what's behind you.
Process information: Using your observations, plan how to deal effectively with the hazards that you have identified.
Give Information: Always give a clear signal when it will assist other road-users. Indicators are the most commonly-used method, but you should also consider arm signals, horn or headlights.

P

POSITION
Once you've considered signals, position your vehicle correctly on the road. Consider a 'Blind Spot Check' before changing course.

S

SPEED
Use your brakes, engine braking or acceleration sense to adjust your speed according to the hazard. Check your mirrors again.

G

GEAR
Once you're travelling at an appropriate speed to negotiate the hazard safely, select the correct gear. (Sometimes, you may need to change gear just before you finish braking.) Consider a 'Blind Spot Check'.

A

ACCELERATION
As soon as your motorcycle is on a straight course after the hazard, accelerate to an appropriate speed.

(Vertical label: INFORMATION)

IPSGA can be applied to any riding situation or manoeuvre. Practise it and IPSGA will soon become a natural thing to do.

It is intended to be used in sequence, with the Information element (in red above) overlapping the other four. If the circumstances change, go back to the beginning and restart IPSGA at the appropriate point. All aspects should be considered, not just applied slavishly, the aim is to think about a situation rather than react automatically. While it may appear longwinded here, when it's put into practice it soon becomes instinctive.

As well as raising awareness of what's going on around you, it also ensures that your actions won't take other road users by surprise. That said, you should keep an eye on other people to make sure they have seen you and are acting accordingly.

# of riding

INFORMATION
This part of the system should be continuously applied. Check all around you and consider the need for signalling. Maintain good all-round observation, looking out for pedestrians and cyclists as well as other vehicles. Plan your course of action.

POSITION
Check your mirrors and/or carry out a 'Blind Spot Check' if you consider it necessary. Carefully move the machine towards the centre of the road, making note of road width, lane markings and any obstructions.

SPEED
Consider your speed. Check your mirrors and, if necessary, brake progressively to a speed that will enable you to complete the manoeuvre in a controlled and safe manner.

GEARS
Once you're at the right speed, select the appropriate gear. Before turning, consider making a final mirror check and/or carrying out a 'Blind Spot Check'.

ACCELERATE
After you turn, progressively accelerate to an appropriate speed.

Before any manoeuvre, you should consider the need for a 'Blind Spot Check'.

This is just one example of IPSGA. To see how it applies to left turns and roundabouts, turn to Riding techniques in Action on pages 61 and 62.

THE IMPORTANCE OF IPSGA

Practise the IPSGA system regularly and it will soon become second nature. If you can do it instinctively, you'll have more time to concentrate on other elements of your riding

Planned 'IPSGA' riding has many benefits, including saving lives and saving fuel.

Know what is going on around you at all times and give necessary information, letting others know what you intend to do. Effective absorbing, using and giving of information is essential to better riding.

Plan your approach to every junction. Consider slowing down earlier, so that vehicles ahead have time to pull away before you arrive. Taking in and processing information throughout any manoeuvre is essential. You aren't going to miss that fast-moving orange truck, but what about the motorcyclist following it?

Early planning and correct gear selection lets you maintain total control on your approach to a junction.

Plan your approach to every junction. Consider slowing down earlier, so that the vehicles ahead have time to pull away before you arrive.

Taking in and processing information throughout any manoeuvre is essential. You aren't going to miss this fast-moving orange truck, but what about the vehicle tucked in behind it?

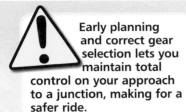

Early planning and correct gear selection lets you maintain total control on your approach to a junction, making for a safer ride.

"Each element of IPSGA should not be applied slavishly, but always be considered."

Know what is going on around you at all times and give necessary information, letting others know what you intend to do. The effective absorbing, using and giving of information is an essential part of an advanced rider's skill-set.

RIDER CHECKLIST
- Use the planned system of riding (IPSGA) every time you change speed or direction.
- Use your mirrors and 'blind spot checks' effectively.
- Signal, where necessary, for the benefit of other road users, including pedestrians.
- Plan your application of the system.
- Remember the maxim: 'Gears to go, brakes to slow.'

EXAMINER CHECKLIST
- Does the rider use the system (IPSGA) consistently throughout the ride?
- Does the rider think about its application or are the stages just slavishly applied?
- Are the mirrors and 'blind spot checks' used appropriately?
- Is the rider aware of the situation both in front of and behind them?
- Does the rider show good hazard awareness and prioritise accordingly?
- Are signals given only when necessary and at the correct time and place?
- Is the IPSGA riding system planned and acted upon in good time?
- Is braking, steering and gear changing systematic and separated?

Observation

Perfecting your vision and observation will keep you out of trouble on Britain's busy roads. Improving your observation takes commitment, consideration and lots of practice

Every junction requires effective observation

Effective observation is a key element of better riding. It will give you time to plan ahead and spot potential hazards before they become a serious problem. Most people's eyesight deteriorates very gradually as they get older. Poor eyesight can affect reaction times and spatial awareness, while restricted peripheral vision may cause you to completely miss a hazard. It's a good idea to have an eye test every two years (or whenever you suspect there's been a deterioration in your vision) and always wear spectacles or contact lenses if an optician has recommended you wear them for riding

To improve your riding, you must try to absorb as much information as possible every time you head out. There are dozens of things going on at any given moment and you have to instantly process all that information, focusing on things that are relevant and disregarding those that are not. Of course, everyone does this to a degree, but develop this skill and you can take your

The chevrons are bordered by broken lines, so you could overtake legally. But did you notice the obscured exit?

riding to another level entirely.

Constantly assess riding conditions, read the road a long distance ahead and make decisions accordingly.

FORWARD OBSERVATION

It might surprise you to know that many riders only focus on the road five to 20 metres in front of them. This means they could miss some dangers altogether or be left with less than a second to react when a hazard suddenly appears.

The key is to constantly scan the area closest to you, as well as the middle distance and all the way to the horizon.

One useful technique is to scan the next section of road, as far as you can see ahead, every time you round a bend or reach the crest of a hill. This early-warning system has massive benefits; you can often see what direction the road is going to take, identify up-coming hazards, see traffic jams early or spot potentially dangerous riders or drivers.

This is possible because, if you look far ahead, you can still be aware of what is happening close to you. But if you look at something very close to you, like the rear of a machine you are following, you will struggle to see ahead.

Careful choice of road positioning is an important element of observation. For example, if you position your bike further back and slightly to the side of traffic ahead and lift your vision, you will be aware of the foreground and also get early warning that the queue of traffic ahead is braking.

Lifting your vision towards the horizon is one of the key techniques of advanced riding.

Many riders have a very narrow field of vision...

...while advanced riders take in information from all around them

REAR OBSERVATION AND CHECKING FOR BLIND SPOTS

In this book, the phrase 'Rear Observation' is a generic term relating to any rearwards observation, either in the mirrors or over the shoulder.

A 'Blind Spot Check' is considered to be a look over the appropriate shoulder to check the area not covered by your mirrors. This observation updates the 'Information' part of your riding 'System'.

It is not meant to be a thorough 180-degree look to the rear, more a quick glance to fill in any blanks left by your mirrors. It is also not intended to replace or replicate normal use of the mirrors, as their use has the advantage of allowing you to maintain a peripheral view of the road ahead whilst looking behind.

The level of vision your mirrors afford affects the frequency with which these checks need to be carried out and this should be considered part of the continuing 'Information' stage of IPSGA.

As with every other part of IPSGA, they should be considered and not just slavishly undertaken. This in turn promotes a 'thinking approach' to your riding in the same way as considering whether a signal is actually needed for every manoeuvre.

Remember that if a 'Blind Spot Check' is required, it must be executed before the manoeuvre, to allow time to react to anything observed.

In addition, 'Blind Spot Checks' should be avoided while in the 'Overtaking Position' (page 75) in case the

The road is clear. Or is it? Always check for blind spots

vehicle ahead brakes while the rider is looking away.

You can obtain much more information from your mirrors with two-observations timed closely together. This enables you to calculate the speed of approach of vehicles by noting any increase in their apparent size, without, of course, neglecting what's happening on the road ahead.

SELECTIVE OBSERVATION

Arguably, the most important part of advanced riding is observation. Riders with effective observation skills have to process lots of information quickly, so it's essential to develop a way of distinguishing between useful and irrelevant information. Here are some useful tips:

- Has the driver on the left at the junction ahead seen you? If you're not sure, move slightly towards the middle of the road, observing oncoming traffic and reducing speed if you feel it's appropriate. Be ready to brake if necessary.
- Watch pedestrians carefully, especially children, OAPs (who may be deaf or partially sighted) and anyone walking a dog. Always be prepared for the unexpected.

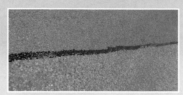

- Changes in a road surface can have dramatic effects on motorcycle control. Look out for mud near farms, fields or construction sites; wet leaves on the road; streams of water running across the highway or even a change in the type of road material: Tarmac, concrete, ShellGrip or slippery overbanding (the low-grip mastic seam between Tarmac joints – see above). All of these can upset a machine's balance.
- A cluster of lamp posts in the distance may give early warning of a roundabout or major junction.
- In busy urban environments, use shop window reflections to observe approaching vehicles or changing traffic lights before you can see them directly.
- Observe parked vehicles ahead to see if there are any occupants. Be aware that a door may suddenly open. If the engine's running (look at the exhaust and lights) consider that the vehicle might suddenly pull out.
- Telegraph poles are often positioned on verges and therefore follow the course of the road. Use them as an early warning system as to the twists and turns the road will take.

Don't rely on them entirely, as they may track across a field (which you don't want to do!)

● Pay extra attention to stationary vans and give them

a wide berth. Delivery vans stop often and someone might get out without looking.

● Watch out for any slow moving vehicles, such as tractors and milk floats or drivers travelling very slowly while looking for an entrance. Due to their slow speed, they can turn without warning.

● Look ahead for pedestrians' feet under the front or rear bumpers of parked vans, lorries and 4x4s. Is someone about to step out into the road?

● When behind a bus or school coach, be aware that when passengers start moving around inside, it's likely that a bus stop is coming up. Drop back ready to see if a safe overtake is possible.

● On hills, a cloud of exhaust smoke from an HGV suggests that it is changing down a gear and may be travelling much more slowly than other traffic.

● As you approach a large vehicle coming towards you, be aware that impatient drivers behind it may attempt dangerous overtakes.

● In bad weather look out for pedestrians whose vision may be limited by umbrellas, coat hoods/parkas or driving rain.

● Notice whether the driver in

front is paying attention. Allow sloppy or aggressive drivers/riders more room. Drop further back from drivers attempting risky overtaking manoeuvres or who seem distracted from their driving.

● Look through breaks in hedges and fences to spot upcoming potential hazards.

● When riding at night, use other vehicles' headlight beams to assess their whereabouts, direction of travel and speed.

● Headlamp beams of other vehicles may also indicate where the road goes next.

Road signs

It is important to know what all road signs mean and update your knowledge from time to time with a glance through the Highway Code. Road signs are the shape they are because, even if you can't see the sign clearly, say in fog or heavy rain, you'll still know when you see a triangular sign that there may be a significant hazard ahead.

So, do you recognise all the signs on this page?

ROAD SIGN RULES

- All warning signs are triangular.
- Advisory signs are rectangular.
- Round signs are 'the law' – you must do what they say.

Road signs are always there for a reason, so don't ignore them. They provide advanced information to help you avoid danger. You should be extra vigilant about some signs, like those warning of schools nearby, as they may indicate a 20mph speed limit ahead. A pole with two or more signs on it should be read from the top. In the example below, you can see that the first bend comes shortly before the junction.

Above: A typical road junction in the UK is home to numerous road signs of all types. You need to know what they all mean

RIDER CHECKLIST
- Develop your selective observation. What information should you act on and what can you ignore?
- Read and understand the meaning of every road sign.
- Use rear-view mirrors to observe where other traffic is and how fast it's travelling.
- Watch the traffic in front of the car you're following. This will give you early warning of potential hazards and general traffic movements.
- Observe activity in the middle-distance, as far as you can see ahead and scan laterally all around you.
- Get your eyes tested every two years or the moment you suspect any deterioration in your vision.

EXAMINER CHECKLIST
- Are mirrors used properly before signalling and manoeuvring?
- Are mirrors used frequently and effectively?
- Does the rider see, absorb and act on all road-sign information?
- Does the rider lift their vision to the road ahead and show good anticipation?
- Are speed and distance judged accurately?
- Can the rider stop in the distance seen to be clear at all times?

Riding plans

Riding plans are a key element of the IPSGA system. How you assess what's going on around you, and how you act on that information is pivotal in taking your riding to the next level

RIDING PLANS: THREE SIMPLE QUESTIONS

WHAT CAN BE SEEN?
Plan your ride on what you can see ahead, to the rear, and all around you.

WHAT CANNOT BE SEEN?
Remember that danger can exist on every hidden section of road: in concealed junctions, driveways, around the next bend or even from a bridge above the road you're on!

What can be seen? The parked lorry causes the 4x4 to make a potentially dangerous manoeuvre

What can't be seen? A hidden roadsign can distract as you try to see the warning

WHAT MIGHT REASONABLY BE EXPECTED TO HAPPEN?
Keep a look-out for clues to dangers that may lay ahead:
- Junction warning signs give early notice that a driver may be waiting to pull out ahead.
- Dustbins outside houses on a twisty road, mean that there could be a stationary dustbin lorry around the next bend and workers in the road.
- Loose hedge clippings or straw on a country road warn that there could be a slow moving tractor or combine harvester round the bend.
- At night, a car's headlight beams will provide early warning of its arrival.
- Think about the actions of the traffic you are following.
- Will that dump truck be turning into the construction site up ahead? Will there be mud on the road? Is it overloaded? Could something fall off it right in front of you?
- Will that brewery lorry pull in suddenly at the next pub?
- Don't follow buses too closely or you may get stuck behind them when they pull up at the next stop. Drop back and keep a look-out for the next stop, as it provides early warning of an opportunity to pass.
- Always be aware that other riders and drivers could (and probably will) do something unexpected at any time. For example, lane discipline on major roundabouts is generally poor and vehicles often swap lanes without any warning.
- Prioritise hazards in order of importance and deal with each one accordingly.

What might reasonably be expected to happen? These school children could run out at any second

With these potential hazards in mind, always ride within the limits of what you can see. Advanced riders never assume anything and always remain alert for danger to emerge from obscured areas. Their constant planning ahead and highly-tuned anticipation skills ensure that they always have a 'Plan B' should the worst-case scenario become a reality.

RIDER CHECKLIST
- Plan your ride. Assess all riding information and act on it.
- Observe others. Anticipate and plan for their actions.
- Allow for your own and other drivers'/riders' reaction times in varying riding conditions.

EXAMINER CHECKLIST
- Is there an awareness of riding plans?
- Are all road and traffic hazards coped with safely and in good time?
- Does the rider concentrate properly and avoid distraction?
- Is courtesy displayed at all times during the ride?
- Is the ride positive?
- Are other vehicles followed at a safe distance?
- Are other road users' reaction times allowed for?

Steering

Effective steering is an essential skill for the advanced rider. The technicalities of steering could fill this book, however there's a simple technique that every rider should know - positive steering. This improves control, allowing any rider to corner more safely, smoothly and progressively

POSITIVE STEERING

For a motorcycle to get round a corner or bend, there needs to be some positive input from the rider. In view of this, and to avoid possible confusion, we will describe that input as 'Positive Steering'.

Above a certain speed, somewhere around 10-15mph, to make a motorcycle/scooter lean in the intended direction of travel the rider needs to put a forward steering input into the handlebars on the side that he or she intends to turn. For example, to turn right the rider needs to push forward on the right handlebar. This will cause the bike to lean to the right and enable it to negotiate the bend. For higher speeds and tighter bends more lean and therefore more initial steering input is needed.

A great deal of the skill of cornering is learning how to use 'Positive Steering' input and how to maintain proper lean angles through the turn.

If a rider is forced, in an emergency, to swerve, it is essential to know, through practice, how to achieve this.

Accidents often result when otherwise experienced riders, who have never developed this skill, encounter an unexpected obstacle and don't instinctively know how to react to it.

Many handling problems are caused by the rider gripping too tightly on the handlebars, thereby adding the inertia of their shoulders, upper body and arms to the steering input.

"Many handling problems are caused by the rider gripping the handlebars too tightly."

Certain machines by their very design require less effort to steer around a bend than others. Notice the rider of the trail-style bike has an almost perfect angle between his forearms and the fork leg and this, combined with the leverage effect of wide handlebars, means that relatively little input is necessary from the rider to achieve the angle of lean necessary to negotiate a bend.

On a sports bike, notice how, when sitting upright with locked elbows, a very inefficient angle is created between the forearms and the front forks. A lot of steering input is wasted pushing down on the handlebars. Add relatively narrow handlebars into the equation and lot of input is needed to change direction. This quickly leads to fatigue, pain and stiffness.

In this picture, the riding position is correct. The angle between the forearms and the fork legs is now far more effective and this in turn will also make any steering inputs more precise and efficient. On a long journey the reduced physical effort needed to turn will result in a more relaxed rider with more concentration left to apply to their riding plan.

INSTINCT VERSUS POSITIVE STEERING

If you have only learnt to steer instinctively around bends, you do so unaware of exactly how you are achieving the bank angle necessary to negotiate that curve effectively. Although you are steering (you wouldn't get round the bend if you weren't) it is not a positive action on your part.

Misjudge the entry speed into a bend even slightly and you might think your only option is braking. But braking could cause the machine to run wide, going off the road or, worse, still, into oncoming traffic.

Utilising positive steering gives you the option to increase the angle of lean and safely negotiate the corner without the need to reduce speed – providing the level of grip and vision are sufficient.

In order to assist with this positive input, a complementary pull with the other hand can be used to assist when more pressure or control is needed.

So if you need more angle of lean to negotiate a right hand bend, you would push the right handlebar forward while simultaneously pulling back on the left handlebar.

The important point here is to ensure that your inputs are at all times commensurate with the amount of steering actually needed. In order to make accurate, proportional, progressive inputs into the steering, it's important to ensure that your riding position is correct.

There should be a gentle bend in the elbows with a relaxed grip on the handlebars and relaxed shoulders. The angle between your forearms and the fork legs should be

as close to 90 degrees as is reasonable to maximise the efficiency of any positive steering inputs. (see page 39)

Positive steering technique applied to a right-hand turn

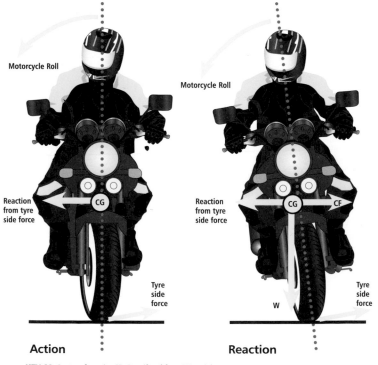

Action **Reaction** **Balance**

KEY CG: Centre of gravity CF: Centrifugal force W: weight

40

QUIET EFFICIENCY – THE HALLMARK OF THE EXPERT

Always aim to steer in a controlled and progressive way, making smooth changes of direction, rather than jerky turns that unbalance your machine. Accurate and smooth steering requires planning and has its roots in motorsport.

Racers recognise that a controlled and smooth ride is ultimately faster and safer than an erratic, jerky one. Sudden steering inputs make for an uncomfortable ride and negate the efforts of the motorcycle's designers to engineer effective suspension and tyres.

For a really smooth ride, focus on your steering, and apply inputs progressively when initiating the lean angle. Maintain a balanced throttle (neither accelerating nor decelerating) through the bend, this makes the most of the machine's grip and poise helping it to hold its line better.

RIDER CHECKLIST
- Always steer smoothly and progressively.
- Hold the handlebars lightly but with a firm grip. This gives maximum feedback from the road and reduces unnecessary steering inputs.
- Don't rely on instinct. Take a proactive approach to steering – apply positive steering inputs counter to the direction you intend to travel.
- Ensure elbows have a slight bend to avoid unwanted steering inputs and to make steering inputs more efficient.

EXAMINER CHECKLIST
- Is steering smooth and accurate?
- Is the rider changing road position and direction smoothly between bends?
- Is the machine positioned properly?
- Are the handlebars held correctly?
- Are the elbows slightly bent?

Positioning

Bikers are almost unique in the motoring world in that they have so much opportunity to use effective positioning, not only to see more, but also to be more visible to others, thereby giving themselves more time to avoid a hazard. The second part of IPSGA is positioning. Having made good use of observation skills to take in all the available information, you then make a mental plan of how to deal with the situation. The first part when carrying out that plan is to consider your best position on the road.

SAFETY POSITION

The 'Safety Position' simply means the most secure place on the road for the rider to occupy, relative to all that is going on around them.

Hazards rarely appear one at a time, they usually occur in combination. Take a typical town scenario: there may be pedestrians on the pavement, a car waiting to emerge from a junction, together with a poor road surface. All these hazards could emerge at once, so the advanced rider must take all this information into account in their plan, and then consider the safest position in the circumstances.

There is no single 'default' safe road position, it varies depending on the situation.

In scenarios where there are both nearside and offside hazards, a centre-of-lane position is likely to be best, depending on the road surface. It also has the advantage that if one of those hazards develops, the rider has the option to move further away from the developing danger.

Advanced riders quickly identify the biggest hazard and give it priority in terms of maintaining a safe distance.

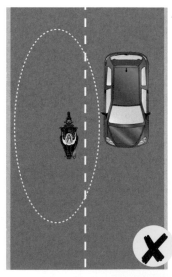

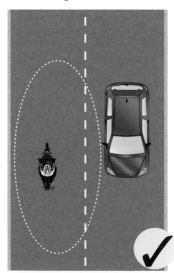

TURNING

When turning into or out of a junction or entrance, it's usually best to be on the left when turning left and on the right when turning right. This makes you less vulnerable from behind, gives following traffic a clearer understanding of where you intend to go and allows you to focus on the real danger, traffic on the road that you are turning into.

VISION

Another advantage of expert positioning, is the ability to see more and in this way obtain more information. This also makes planning more effective.

Obscured nearside road junctions hide approaching vehicles until very late. The further the rider is towards the centre of the road, the more they will be able to see into the junction and the sooner the approaching driver will be able to see them.

Should the unexpected occur, the rider is also further from the danger, so has more time to react appropriately.

Even if a car isn't immediately visible, one could appear at any second, so plan as if it is there.

When approaching a 'T' junction with restricted vision, many drivers, will only give themselves a fraction of a second to see if it is clear to drive onto the major road. In addition they will probably be

looking for another car, not a bike. If the approaching rider is too close to the kerb, they may be obscured among the confusion of parked cars, trees, streetlights or telegraph poles.

Most accidents involving a rider and another vehicle occur at junctions. With effective planning and excellent road positioning, a rider can go a long way towards eliminating the likelihood of these accidents occurring.

The concealed exit looks clear...
but one second later...

Position yourself decisively to the left of the junction when turning left...

...and to the right when turning right

How to be a better rider

IN TOWN

In town, hazards tend to come in multiples, so any positioning needs to take into account all the dangers at any given moment. You need to prioritise the most important hazards so that you can be sure of staying a safe distance from them. This gives you more time to react to the most serious dangers if it becomes necessary, by creating a 'bubble' of comparative safety around you.

Because of the relatively low riding speeds in town, positioning for vision in order to maximise the distance in which you can see becomes less vital. Avoiding danger is the most important thing.

Learner drivers, safety cameras, changing road surfaces: hazards come thick and fast when riding in town

Unnecessary re-positioning, in order to try to gain a better view ahead in such situations, is likely to confuse following traffic and adds an extra element of danger to your ride.

IN THE COUNTRY

On rural roads your riding speeds will almost certainly be higher, so the distance that you can see to be clear ahead becomes far more important. If you double your speed you quadruple your stopping distance, (See page 51) so being able to see well into the distance is vital.

By riding close to the verge, your view is very limited through this bend...

...by moving out safely towards the centre of the road you increase your depth of vision massively

BENDS

Position your bike towards the outside of the bend for the furthest and best view through it. This technique allows you more time to react to hazards, eg: an oncoming vehicle passing a nervous horse, or a static queue of traffic.

Looking further ahead is a priority at higher speeds, but you should not compromise your safety through poor positioning. For example, it could be dangerous to ride close to the nearside edge of the road in order to get a better view into a right-hand bend, only to find yourself in danger from a car emerging out of a junction.

When adopting a 'vision line' – a line that gives you the best view – in bends, hold that position throughout the bend until you can see the exit – unless there is some other danger that requires you to modify the line. Plan your exit from this bend so that you move seamlessly into the best position to handle the next hazard.

Your position on the exit of the bend will depend on what the next hazard is, and, even if you know what sort of bend follows, there may be a new hazard such as stationary traffic or diesel on the road to contend with.

Only by waiting until you can clearly see the exit will you know what awaits you.

Finally, remember to use the 'Limit Point' to control your speed in the bend (see page 68).

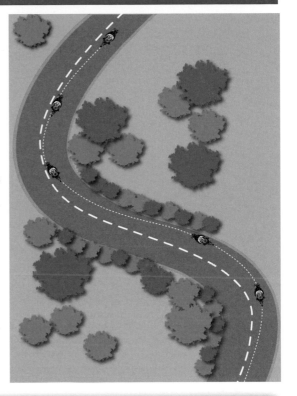

FOLLOWING VEHICLES

When following traffic, the comparatively high position of a rider means that they can often see over the roof of cars as well as through the windows.

Where this is not possible, such as with a truck or bus, it's important to position far enough back so that you can see past either side of the vehicle ahead with just a small change of position.

When following a large vehicle round a left-hand bend, positioning well back means you can see further ahead by looking down the nearside of the vehicle. The same goes for right-hand bends, by looking down the offside of the vehicle.

RIDER CHECKLIST
● **Always place yourself in the safest position on the road taking into account ALL that is going on around you.**
● **Position yourself for the best view only when it is genuinely advantageous. If you are going slowly, you gain little advantage, but can confuse other drivers.**
● **When speeds are low, prioritise hazard avoidance ahead of seeking greater forward vision.**
● **When turning at junctions, position yourself to reduce your vulnerability from following traffic – generally left when turning left, right when turning right.**
● **When deciding where to position, always take into account the road surface and the grip available.**

EXAMINER CHECKLIST
● **Does the rider take a 'thinking' approach to their positioning?**
● **Does the rider prioritise hazards and position accordingly?**
● **Is positioning carried out confidently and decisively?**
● **Does the rider obstruct other drivers with poor positioning?**
● **Does the rider leave themselves vulnerable to following traffic or mislead traffic through poor positioning when turning?**
● **Does the rider confuse following traffic by positioning for vision at low speeds when there is little real benefit?**

Speed and acceleration

Knowing when to use your machine's power and when to ease off are skills that every good rider must master. The IAM's Skill For Life isn't about riding around at a snail's pace, it's about using your bike's power and acceleration smoothly and safely

WISE USE OF POWER

Power is nothing without control. This is true of all aspects of riding, and a good maxim to apply.

Never abuse your motorcycle's power. Instead learn how the engine delivers its power, then use your experience to make the most of it, riding as safely and smoothly as possible.

Firm acceleration is sometimes necessary – when joining a motorway from a slip-road or when overtaking, for example – but to make the best use of your machine's power takes practice and an understanding of the way the engine delivers its torque (the force that creates acceleration).

Being in the wrong gear at the wrong time can 'bog' the engine down, restricting the bike's acceleration and possibly putting you in a hazardous situation (see page 56 on use of gears). It's important to learn which part of the rev band delivers the most torque and

acceleration. This will ensure that you select the right gear for the conditions and situation.

Different engine capacities deliver power differently. You may need to be in a lower gear to 'hit' the power band on a modern multi-cylinder sports machine. Typically, you might need to make use of third gear to accelerate on a short motorway slip road.

Large capacity twins on the other hand, generally produce their torque lower down the rev range. This reduces the need for changing down, but does mean that twins run out of their power band much earlier than their multi-cylinder equivalents, necessitating earlier up-changes to make good progress.

Modern fuel-injected engines do not consume petrol when the throttle is off. Therefore, using the block changing or short-shifting techniques described on page 57 can save both money and the planet.

ACCELERATED LEARNING

Advanced riders with well-developed 'Acceleration Sense' use their brakes much less than ordinary riders.

Through good observation and anticipation, and excellent planning, they quickly assess the situation ahead and make the necessary changes to their speed to produce a progressive, smooth and safe ride.

Skilful use of the throttle makes for a smooth ride and saves fuel

They always use the throttle progressively. For firm acceleration, they begin by accelerating moderately, then, once the machine is settled, they apply more throttle.

They use the same technique when decelerating, easing off the throttle gradually at first, to produce a more controlled, smooth and economical ride.

The displayed speed limit is the maximum speed you should ride at. In this congested situation, 20mph would be too fast

TEST YOUR SENSE OF ACCELERATION

Here's a useful way to test your sense of acceleration or deceleration. Next time you're travelling at the national speed limit and see a 30 or 40mph speed limit sign ahead, try to time the point at which you close the throttle, so that your motorcycle reaches the speed limit sign at the correct speed, without touching the brakes.

On twisty roads you can take this technique a stage further, by managing the speed of your machine between bends with accurate use of the throttle in an appropriate gear. This limits the amount of braking you need to do, producing a smoother, more satisfying ride, it will also make you a more precise rider and you'll save fuel. See page 68 for further information on the 'Limit Point of Vision', another useful tool to help develop your 'acceleration sense'.

> "For maximum stability and comfort, keep a balanced throttle"

ACCELERATING ON BENDS

A motorcycle is most stable when it is travelling in a straight line under progressive, smooth acceleration.

Things can go wrong when the machine is banked in a turn and the rider accelerates too harshly or erratically.

For maximum stability and comfort, maintain a 'balanced-throttle' at a constant speed whilst holding a smooth line through the bend.

(See Cornering on page 68).

ACCELERATION AND OVERTAKING

Make sure all your overtaking manoeuvres are carried out safely, smoothly and swiftly.

If you have to push your machine to the limit, or other road users have to take avoiding action, it means you've left too small a safety margin. Select the best gear for the overtake, bearing in mind your machine's power delivery, to ensure it will produce the acceleration required.

Avoid changing gear during the move, as it increases the time you're exposed to danger.

SPEED

Spot speed limit changes early using your observation skills, and stay in a gear that will help you to remain at a legal speed. For example, when riding in town at 30mph, third gear (depending on the engine type) is often a good choice as it delivers decent acceleration when you need it, whilst at the same time allowing you to slow just by closing the throttle.

Speed limits show you the maximum speed you can drive at. In busy urban environments or anywhere with lots of potential hazards – a busy city street with lots of parked vehicles, or outside a school or hospital – it may be advisable to ride considerably slower.

With smooth road surfaces and powerful, quiet machines, it can sometimes take serious concentration not to creep over the speed limit.

One of the 'Golden Rules' is to always ride at a speed that allows you to stop safely in the distance you can see to be clear on your own side of the road. Never be pressured into breaking the speed limit by the vehicles behind you.

> ⚠ Always ride at a speed where you can stop in the distance you can see to be clear on your side of the road.

Riders who tootle along at 50mph on a busy motorway or 30mph on a clear country road can be as dangerous and frustrating as those riding too fast. Make good progress wherever possible by carrying out well-timed overtakes; smooth, progressive cornering and controlled acceleration.

RIDER CHECKLIST
● Familiarise yourself with your machine's power delivery, so that you can make the best use of the power available.
● Make sure you're in the correct gear and use as much power as is safe when overtaking.
● Accelerate smoothly and progressively, but with economy in mind.
● Develop your 'acceleration sense'. You'll use your brakes less, know instinctively when an overtake is on and ride altogether more smoothly.
● Use a balanced throttle to keep the manoeuvre stable and smooth.

EXAMINER CHECKLIST
● Are speed limits adhered to?
● Is the use of acceleration excessive or insufficient?
● Is acceleration smooth and progressive?
● Is acceleration used at the right time and place, yet with economy in mind?
● Does the rider make good progress and exercise proper restraint?
● Is the balance of the machine maintained in bends?

Braking

If you've ever been a 'nodding-dog' passenger on the back of a bike and got off feeling sick, you'll know the effects of poor, ill-timed and harsh braking.

Taking the time to develop a smooth, progressive and effective braking technique makes every ride safer and more pleasurable... for everyone!

SMOOTHNESS

The trick to smooth braking is to always aim to decelerate progressively and smoothly. You can achieve this by developing your observation and anticipation skills, as these prepare you to brake earlier if any unexpected hazards arise.

Really effective braking is a skill that requires practice. For the most effective results you should apply pressure to the brake lever progressively, aiming to do most of your braking in the middle part, then roll off the brake again and select the best gear appropriate to your speed.

This method produces the smoothest, most effective performance. Try it out by aiming to achieve a smooth ride with such gradual deceleration that your passenger doesn't even realise you are braking.

Well-timed braking makes you faster from A to B. Take timing your arrival at a roundabout for example. Look well ahead and assess the traffic on the roundabout, then time your arrival so that you don't have to stop. Other bikes that passed you as you were decelerating early will be at a standstill trying to find first gear as you slide effortlessly past and get straight back on the throttle.

Planning your braking early makes for a smoother more consistent ride and saves fuel.

BRAKING DISTANCE

Total stopping distance is worked out by adding 'thinking distance' and 'braking distance' together. The time it takes you to react is the main factor in 'thinking distance'. 'Braking distance' will vary according to your speed, the road surface, your machine's weight and the condition of its suspension, brakes and especially its tyres.

Remember, as your speed doubles, your stopping distance will actually quadruple!

The fractions of a second that it takes to get your fingers on the brake lever could be crucial

Keep your foot over the rear brake pedal when there are developing hazards

"Remember, as your speed doubles, your stopping distance will quadruple!"

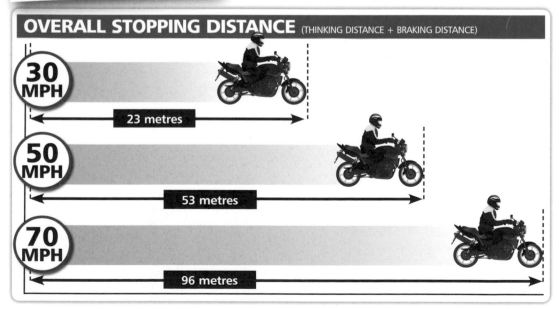

OVERALL STOPPING DISTANCE (THINKING DISTANCE + BRAKING DISTANCE)

30 MPH — 23 metres

50 MPH — 53 metres

70 MPH — 96 metres

Braking distances increase significantly in the wet, especially at speed.

One of the biggest factors in effective wet braking is the quality of your tyres.

You should always invest as much as you can afford to buy the best tyres possible.

Also, always make sure you have plenty of even tread on your tyres. The legal minimum

is 1.0mm, but consider renewing your tyres well before they reach that low a level, as lack of tread and profile massively effects wet braking, steering response and handling.

How to be a better rider

JUDGING DISTANCE

It is essential that you maintain a sensible distance between your bike and the vehicle in front. Under normal riding conditions, this is considered to be two seconds. To measure it, watch as the vehicle you are following passes a fixed point, say a bridge or shadow across the road. Start counting immediately ('one, one thousand, two, one thousand'). If you reach that point before two seconds has elapsed, you are too close.

On motorways and some dual-carriageways, you can use the white distance marker posts, positioned every 100 metres along the side of the road, to judge safe distance.

If the vehicle behind you is too close, you should leave extra distance in front of you to give yourself more braking time. In effect, you are braking for the vehicle behind you.

The same is true if you see an old or poorly-maintained vehicle looming in your mirrors. Its brakes are unlikely to be as effective as yours, so sudden braking on your part could cause it to run right into you!

However tempting it may be, don't react aggressively to tailgaters, simply let them pass

as soon as possible. Also bear in mind that many modern vehicles have complex anti-lock braking systems that require very little in the way of driver skill to operate, even in poor conditions. Most motorcycles and scooters don't have this advantage, so it's all down to the skill of the rider.

BRAKE IN A STRAIGHT LINE

Even if your bike has ABS (anti-lock brake system), you should carry out firm braking in a straight line, as using your brakes mid-bend can upset the balance of the bike.

If you have to brake mid-corner, do so progressively, avoid locking the wheels and use positive steering. Whenever possible, avoid using the front brake when banked over.

As the most effective braking happens just before the wheels lock-up, try to develop a feel for this moment, and vary the brake pressure according to the road surface and conditions.

Only ever practise emergency braking in a safe place like on an old airfield. Even firm braking should be done progressively, keeping the ride as smooth as possible.

Do your braking in a straight line before a bend – it keeps your bike stable

"Only a fool breaks the two-second rule!"
Try it, it takes two seconds to say

Two seconds

One second

Think! If the driver in front hits the brakes hard with all that ABS technology working for them, could you stop in time?

ANTI-LOCK BRAKES

Anti-lock brake systems (ABS) help prevent a bike's wheels from locking-up in an emergency situation.

ABS works by releasing the brakes just before the wheel locks up, then quickly reapplies them. This process can be repeated hundreds of times every second, which means that the wheel never actually locks up. It is quite normal for these pulses to be felt through the brake lever, so you should maintain your braking pressure.

Don't let ABS lull you into a false sense of security though. Ideally your observation and anticipation will mean that you never need to rely on ABS.

"Don't let ABS lull you into a false sense of security. Good observation means you never rely on it"

EMERGENCY BRAKING

Braking as firmly as you can on an ABS-equipped machine is generally the quickest way to stop in the dry. In wet or slippery conditions, a machine fitted with ABS may take longer to stop as the ABS works hard to maintain stability.

Due to its comparatively short wheelbase, braking hard on any machine, and especially on a sports bike, results in a large amount of weight transference to the front tyre. The more weight on the tyre, the more grip it will have on the road. If you apply all the braking input before that load has transferred to the front end, i.e: 'snatch' at the brakes, the front wheel is likely to lock quite easily even in dry conditions. However, if you brake progressively, you will allow time for the front suspension to compress, weight transference to take place and you'll be surprised at just how much extra braking can be achieved before any skidding takes place.

Conversely, with most weight transferred to the front wheel, there is much less on the back-end. This means the rear locks far more easily, so less pedal pressure should be used.

In an emergency scenario, you don't have time to practise, so correct braking technique has to be developed beforehand to the point where it is instinctive.

Many local IAM groups actually run day courses to help riders practise this invaluable skill, make use of them.

Even with quick reactions, it can take over half-a-second to get your hand/foot on to the brake

BRAKE FAILURE

Modern braking systems are very reliable, so total brake failure is extremely rare, but it can still sometimes occur.

A slow hydraulic leak will make the brake lever feel spongy and the brakes will start to lose their 'bite'. You may need to pump your brake lever or pedal repeatedly to restore pressure in order to get any braking-effect back. If you recognise these symptoms, have your brakes checked immediately by a mechanic, before riding again.

In very wet conditions, during a storm or after riding through a forded river, check your brakes. Apply them progressively, but firmly, to clear any water from between the pad and disc.

Should total brake failure occur on one brake, use the other, and/or quickly change

down through the gears (whilst steering in a straight line) for maximum braking effect.

Brake progressively and consistently to make the most of smooth sweeping bends like these

BRAKE FADE

When riding progressively on twisty country roads, and particularly on steep downhill sections, your bike could suffer from brake fade.

This happens when your brake discs and pads get very hot from repeated use and begin to lose their effectiveness. In extreme circumstances, the brake fluid can actually boil leading to total brake failure.

It's worth noting that while this is very unlikely to happen on modern machines, brake fade can affect older bikes, especially those with drum brakes. To restrain the bike's speed, select a low gear to go down steep hills and use engine braking to slow the bike. Even consider the use of the engine cut-out switch.

RIDER CHECKLIST
- Always test your brakes before starting out on a journey.
- Allow for the reactions of other drivers when you brake.
- Know your bike's braking ability. Always stay well within the limits of the bike (and your own riding ability).
- When braking firmly, do it in a straight line as it keeps the bike stable.
- Always consider your total stopping distance.
- Brake smoothly and progressively at all times.

EXAMINER CHECKLIST
- Is braking smooth and progressive?
- Are mirrors and signals used prior to braking where appropriate?
- Are road and weather conditions taken into account?
- Does a lack of planning mean the rider has to brake twice when approaching a hazard?
- Does the rider avoid overlapping gear, brake and steering inputs?

Changing gears

Smooth, efficient use of a bike's gearbox is an essential skill to master, as it increases motorcycle control, performance, economy and comfort

SMOOTH USE OF GEARS AND CLUTCH

A good gear change can be so smooth that any pillion passenger you carry won't even notice that it has taken place.

To achieve this smoothness you must select a gear that is appropriate to your engine speed and road speed, and you must use the throttle and clutch skilfully. Your goal should be to ride as smoothly as possible at all times.

Riders often get a false perception of how smooth their riding is because they have the handlebars for support. Ask your passenger for an assessment of your riding smoothness. If they are sliding about or there is a clashing of helmets regularly, your technique isn't smooth enough and needs more work.

As a general rule when

changing up a gear, shut the throttle and pull in the clutch simultaneously, then only reapply the throttle as your hand is releasing the clutch. Expert timing will produce silky smooth changes every time.

When changing down a gear, you'll increase smoothness by matching engine speed and

road speed with a blip of the throttle while the clutch is in.

Smooth gear changes are also good for your bike (and wallet) by keeping your clutch and gearbox in top condition for longer and saving petrol. Poor gear changes and 'riding the clutch' cause expensive premature wear.

GET THE RIGHT GEAR

Always select a gear that balances your need for economy, performance and mechanical sympathy.

For demanding roads/traffic situations keep the engine revs near the middle of the power band so that your throttle is immediately effective for acceleration or deceleration.

For less demanding roads or quiet traffic situations a higher gear minimises wear and improves fuel economy.

You should always aim to minimise mechanical inputs. For example, after a fast third-gear overtake, it can sometimes be best to block-change into fifth or sixth gear (see next page). Selecting too high a gear causes the engine to 'bog down', killing acceleration. Slick, well-timed gear changes drop you nicely into the power band for the next gear, ensuring both good progress and economy.

Minimise these negative issues by learning your engine's power-delivery characteristics. Knowing how it performs will produce a smoother, faster and more economical ride.

Use engine braking for steep hill descents by selecting a lower gear. This reduces strain on your brakes.

As a general rule, use the same gear to descend a hill as you would to ride up it. This delivers a good braking effect.

Correct lever position improves reaction times and comfort on long rides

BLOCK CHANGING GEARS

This is an advanced technique for quickly changing through the gears after heavy braking or rapid acceleration.

You block change by pulling in the clutch as normal, then moving the gear lever through multiple gears – either up or down – before releasing the clutch again once you're in your chosen gear.

For instance, if you accelerate rapidly to the speed limit in third gear, why change through fourth and fifth to sixth gear just to maintain the same speed? Minimise your riding inputs and fuel consumption by block changing straight into sixth gear from third.

Conversely, on approaching a roundabout or junction, slow down using your acceleration sense or brakes, then block change straight into the best gear for your exit – say from sixth gear to second gear – in a single, quick action.

ECO RIDING

The IAM has recognised the value of economical riding to the motorcyclist and the environment for many years.

Understanding your machine's power delivery and where its powerband lies is essential to maximise both economy and performance. This allows you to get the most out of your engine at all times.

These techniques deliver a fuel-efficient and therefore environmentally-friendly ride.

RIDER CHECKLIST
- All gear changes should be smooth, precise and well-timed.
- Where appropriate, select gears with economy and the environment in mind.
- Smooth, slick down-changes require the ability to match engine and road speeds.
- Use your gears to control speed on steep hills and in slippery conditions.
- Overtaking requires a planned gear-changing technique.

EXAMINER CHECKLIST
- Is the rider in the correct gear for every situation? (Consider Eco riding)
- Are engine and road speeds correctly synchronised when changing gear?
- Is the rider using block changing where appropriate?
- Are gears changed smoothly?
- Is the hand off the clutch between changes?
- Are the gears being used to replace braking?

Riding economically

The average British family now spends more money on its vehicles and transportation than it does on food. More than ever, it pays dividends to ride with economy in mind.

With the cost of owning a bike going up each year, it makes total sense to ride economically.

ECONOMICAL AND ECO-FRIENDLY RIDING TIPS

With everything from fuel and insurance, to parts and labour costing more each year, it makes sense to ride as economically and with as much 'mechanical sympathy' as possible.

The IAM has always embraced this philosophy. Smooth, progressive riding results in savings in fuel and component wear. This doesn't mean you have to ride everywhere slowly – skilled riders make good progress, but they do so using good planning which in turn uses less fuel and reduces tyre and machine wear and tear.

Using less fuel not only saves money but also helps to save the planet. Here are some useful tips to cut both your expenditure and the CO_2 you pump into the atmosphere.

- Planning ahead as you ride not only makes you much more aware of hazards, it also helps you to ride smoothly, progressively and economically.
- Use acceleration sense. Do you go straight from the throttle to the brake? You can save significant amounts of fuel by planning ahead and gently letting your engine deceleration bring you to a halt.
- Block changing (page 57) uses your engine's power most efficiently and saves fuel.
- Obey speed limits. Riding smoothly at the speed limit will use less fuel. Typically, riding at 70mph uses 20 per cent less fuel than riding at 85mph.
- Intelligent filtering (see page 81) saves both time and fuel and is one of the big advantages riding has over driving in our crowded cities.
- In a traffic jam, if the option to filter isn't there, let the vehicle in front open up a gap then try to keep moving smoothly rather than stopping and starting unnecessarily.
- Try to minimise the number of times you have to place a foot on the ground.
- Keep your cruising speed constant with good planning.
- Find out where your machine's power band is (check in the manual). If peak power is at 10,000rpm, for example, don't rev all the way to the rev limiter at 11,000rpm as you'll be wasting fuel and performance.
- Regular servicing maintains engine performance, efficiency and economy. Poorly-serviced machines use more fuel.
- Checking tyre pressures regularly, minimises tread wear and fuel consumption.
- Switch off the engine when stuck in traffic, say, at level crossings and similar, but make sure the situation behind has stabilised first.

SAFETY V ECONOMY

Never put fuel economy ahead of safety.

Riding significantly slower than the conditions demand, for the sake of fuel economy, makes you as much of a hazard as someone riding too fast.

People in the queue behind you may get impatient and take unnecessary risks to overtake.

RIDER CHECKLIST
- A planned ride is an economical ride.
- Good use of acceleration sense, block changing and knowing your machine's power delivery all help to save fuel (and the planet).

EXAMINER CHECKLIST
- Does the rider have a reasonable sense of economy, avoiding excessive revs and unnecessary braking?
- Are low gears held for too long, or is the engine labouring in higher gears?
- Is the rider's planning and anticipation good enough to produce a dividend in economical riding?
- Is the right balance struck between making progress and achieving good economy?

3 // RIDING TECHNIQUES IN ACTION

Road basics

If you master all the fundamental riding techniques to the point where they become second nature, you'll have more time left to hone your skills.
  This chapter explains how to achieve this goal

JUNCTIONS

The majority of bike collisions involving another vehicle occur near T-junctions, crossroads, side turnings or roundabouts.
  Almost all of these are caused by driver or rider error. The majority are not the fault of the rider, they are: "Sorry-mate-I-didn't-see-you" situations, but it's the rider who invariably comes off worse.
  By developing a systematic approach to your riding (IPSGA, page 26), you will massively reduce the likelihood of such an 'accident' happening to you.

⚠ Remember, in the following example IPSGA situations, each stage should be considered and used only where appropriate, not slavishly applied.
  Where mirrors are mentioned, the rider must also consider a 'Blind Spot Check' where necessary.
  Aim to be a thinking rider, not an automaton.

INFORMATION
Use your mirrors and all-round vision to check the movements of other road users. Consider signalling if appropriate.

POSITION
Consider positioning your machine towards the left of the road, and carrying out a 'Blind Spot Check' if necessary

SPEED
Consider checking your mirrors and adjust your speed as necessary to prepare for the turn. Consider a signal and, if necessary, brake progressively. The tighter arc of a left turn generally requires a slower speed than that of a right turn.

GEARS
Once you're at the right speed for the turn, select the correct gear, reconsider a signal before turning, and a final mirror and/or 'Blind Spot Check' where you feel it's appropriate.

ACCELERATE
After the turn, progressively accelerate to an appropriate speed for the conditions.

⚠️ As you approach a left turn, check your depth of vision into the junction. Use this, and the 'limit point of vision' technique, to gauge your entry speed. The nearer your LPOV, the slower you should go. (see LPOV on page 68)

To see IPSGA applied to a right-hand turn, see page 27

How to be a better rider

IPSGA APPLIED TO TURNING RIGHT AT A ROUNDABOUT

INFORMATION
Check your mirrors and use your all-round vision to spot any hazards. Consider a signal to change course.

POSITION
Approach the roundabout according to which exit you plan to take.
   If turning right, consider moving towards the centre of the road. Update your information with a mirror and 'Blind Spot Check' if needed.

SPEED
Decelerate smoothly to a speed that will bring you to the give-way line at the right time to slot smoothly into a gap in the traffic, if vision and conditions allow.

'Brakes are for slowing, gears are for going!' Use this mantra to remind yourself of the correct way to decelerate.
   If closing the throttle is insufficient, use your brakes to slow your machine. Once you're at your target speed, block change into the correct gear to progress.
   Don't use your gearbox to slow yourself down.

GEARS
Once you're at the right speed to enter the roundabout, select the correct gear, and consider a signal and 'Blind Spot Check' before turning.

ACCELERATE
Choose an appropriate gap in the traffic and accelerate smoothly onto the roundabout.
   Check your mirrors frequently and reconsider giving a right-turn signal.
   Always avoid disrupting the flow of traffic.

POSITION
Think about a mirror and 'Blind Spot Check'.
   Reconsider signals, then move to the left-hand lane in time for your exit.

ACCELERATE
As you turn off the roundabout, accelerate smoothly to an appropriate speed, bearing in mind the traffic and road conditions.

ROUNDABOUTS

Generally, the safest course for a bike to take through a roundabout, in the absence of other road users, is the shortest route from entry to exit.

However, for all the examples shown here, we'll assume the presence of other road users.

Correct positioning and signalling are crucial at roundabouts and should always be complemented by a decisive but safe entry into the traffic flow. Calculate the speed and assess the traffic flow on and near the roundabout as you approach. Try to time your arrival with a gap in the traffic, so that you don't have to stop, or obstruct other traffic.

A slightly slower approach often allows unobstructed progress, letting you negotiate and exit a roundabout more quickly than a rider who races up to the line and has to stop.

In light traffic, you should only have to reduce your speed slightly to enter a roundabout, but bear in mind that road-users at the previous entry may be thinking exactly the same thing.

Always be vigilant and never assume that other drivers will do as their signalling suggests.

Always ride in a way that allows you to change your plan if a signal is ignored.

MINI-ROUNDABOUTS

Single mini-roundabouts are rarely a problem, but bunch a series of them together and some road-users seem to lose the plot completely, creating a real hazard.

Approach a cluster of mini-roundabouts one at a time and treat each one individually. They should pose no threat if well planned, other than the need for increased awareness of other road users' behaviour.

Always be safe, observant and decisive, and, where possible, avoid riding onto the central white circle.

When roads are empty, the advanced rider takes the shortest route through the mini-roundabout

SIGNALLING AT ROUNDABOUTS

On standard roundabouts in the presence of other traffic, follow the advice in the Highway Code, unless lane markings instruct otherwise.

Below, you can see some suggested methods for dealing with a complex six-exit roundabout.

TURNING LEFT

Get in the left-hand lane and consider signalling left on your approach. Continue to indicate until you reach your exit.

STRAIGHT OVER

Approach the roundabout in the left lane and stay in that lane once you're on the roundabout. Signal left when you pass the exit before yours.

Observe early to see if the left lane is busy. If it is, consider using the right-hand or centre lane. Use the same technique on the roundabout, but be extra observant, making good use of the mirrors and/or a 'Blind Spot Check' if necessary when exiting.

TURNING RIGHT

Signalling right, take the right-hand lane into the roundabout and stay in that lane once on the roundabout.

As you pass the exit that precedes yours, consider using your mirrors, indicate left and, observing carefully, move across to exit the roundabout.

The number of lanes entering and exiting, affects your approach and signalling.

Use your indicators to confirm your intentions and position your machine decisively.

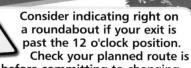

Consider indicating right on a roundabout if your exit is past the 12 o'clock position. Check your planned route is clear before committing to changing lanes to exit. Direction arrows (without mandatory signage) on the approach are for advice only.

How to be a better rider

TURNING RIGHT AT CROSSROADS (OFF THE MAJOR ROUTE)

Turning right at crossroads can be a confusing manoeuvre if an oncoming vehicle is also trying to turn right.

Problems arise if the two drivers treat the manoeuvre differently – one trying to pass nearside-to-nearside, the other offside-to-offside.

Follow the advice in the Highway Code and always try to pass offside-to-offside, past the oncoming vehicle in the junction, in order to turn right behind it. This gives a clearer view of approaching traffic and makes you more visible too.

Occasionally, road markings, traffic conditions or the actions of the oncoming driver, might

Avoid positioning your bike too close behind other vehicles at junctions – see page 86

prevent you from taking this approach, so always proceed decisively, but cautiously, remaining aware that other drivers may not do what you expect them to.

At junctions, is the other driver looking at you and are they aware that you are there?

CROSSROADS AND T JUNCTIONS

At junctions where you are on the minor route, or where neither route has precedence:
- Absorb information regarding junction layout and plan your approach early.
- Where appropriate, stay close to the nearside if you're turning left, and when turning right, stay close to the centre line.
- Check your mirrors, then signal if necessary, before braking early.
- Pay extra attention to your speed, and make sure you hold the correct road position.
- Once stopped at the junction, consider selecting neutral if conditions mean you'll be stationary for a while.
- When turning, it often makes sense to put down the foot that corresponds to the direction you intend turning.

That way your machine is already leaning slightly towards the direction in which you plan to travel. This may subconsciously hint to other road-users which way you intend turning.

- Make sure you are aware of the intentions of drivers at any road opposite before you begin to pull out.
- Always be patient. In heavy traffic, don't take risks by accelerating into too small a gap. Never cause other drivers to brake or swerve.
- As you turn, raise your vision in the direction you intend to ride. If you look initially at the opposite kerb you will end up riding in an unnecessarily wide arc as you turn.
- Don't assume that a flashing indicator means the driver will definitely make the manoeuvre. They may have left it on by accident, they may be confused or intend to take the turn directly after yours.
- Only pull out, when the other driver begins their turn.

If riding on a main road:
- Being on the major route at a junction doesn't mean you can do exactly as you like.

Remember, irrespective of the right of way, a rider is likely to

be the one to suffer most in any collision.

Pay attention to other road users and always expect the worst from them, such as unsignalled manoeuvres, late braking and indecisiveness.
- On a main road, when approaching a junction where a vehicle is waiting, try to observe the driver. Attempt to achieve eye contact but at the same time don't assume that because they are looking in your direction, they've seen you. Consider adjusting your position on the road, to give yourself vital fractions of a second to avoid a collision, should they pull out in front of you unexpectedly. If you are not sure that they have seen you, ease off the throttle and cover your brakes.

Always aim to be considerate, but at the same time never put courtesy ahead of practicality or safety. For example, only let someone out of a junction if it won't cause undue braking by drivers behind you.

TRAFFIC LIGHTS

Good planning at traffic lights can speed up your progress.

Look ahead. If there's a choice of lanes, pick the one with the least traffic or the one with no slow-moving HGV or bus.

Often the inside lane is empty. This gives you a clear run and you won't get held up by traffic stopping to turn right.

Observe the traffic beyond the lights, as lanes often merge. Choose the lane that lets you make the best progress.

Time your arrival at traffic lights for when they're green. If you see a red light ahead, slow down to delay your arrival. This way you won't have to stop.

If you have to stop, do so just before the stop line and consider selecting neutral once the situation behind is clear.

Never pull up too close behind other traffic at lights – always leave enough room to manoeuvre easily around them should they stall or breakdown.

If the lights for the other routes aren't visible, look for signs of the traffic slowing as their lights go to red. Use this anticipation to your advantage.

If you can see the lights controlling the other routes, as soon as they turn amber, consider selecting first gear, as your lights should go green in the next few seconds. Never move off before your lights turn green.

Finally, always be aware of drivers or cyclists running red lights, as this behaviour is increasingly common.

Making planned and well-timed progress on busy urban roads is very satisfying, especially when you slide effortlessly past the high-revving, inconsiderate rider who rocketed by you seconds earlier, only to end up in the wrong lane and wrong gear at the lights.

RIDER CHECKLIST
- Remember all junctions are hazards.
- Always consider signalling well in advance of a manoeuvre and take up the correct road position decisively.
- Pull away from a junction only when it's completely safe to do so.
- If you expect to be stopped at a junction for a while, consider selecting neutral.
- On right turns at crossroads, pass oncoming traffic offside-to-offside before making your right turn. Occasionally road markings or traffic conditions may prevent this.
- Always select the correct lane and signalling procedure when approaching and negotiating roundabouts. Your entry and exit should be decisive, well-observed and safe.

EXAMINER CHECKLIST
- Are signals, signs and road markings observed and obeyed?
- Is the correct road position taken up early when approaching a hazard?
- At a stop sign does the rider come to a complete stop?
- Are roundabouts negotiated safely, with a well-timed approach, good position and considered signalling, plus a confident entry and exit?
- Is sound judgement of gaps in traffic used when negotiating all hazards?

Cornering

Many aspects of motorcycling are exhilarating, but smooth, progressive and safe cornering takes some beating.

Always aim to handle corners in a prepared and precise way, with good observation and planning, an appropriate line through the bend and a progressive exit.

These fundamental skills raise riding standards to a whole new level as even an innocuous-looking corner requires good riding technique to prevent it from becoming a hazard.

WHAT IS THE 'LIMIT POINT' OF VISION?

The 'Limit Point' is the furthest point ahead where you have a clear view of the road surface.

On a clear, level road this is the point at which the two sides of the road appear to meet. Always ride at a speed that lets you stop (on your own side of the road) within the distance you can see is clear – that's the distance between you and the 'Limit Point'.

This then determines how fast you can safely enter a corner.

The closer the 'Limit Point' is, the less time and distance you have in which to act and therefore the slower you need to go – and vice versa.

This applies to junctions as well as bends.

Limit point of vision

Match your speed to the distance the 'Limit Point' is away from you. This ensures you can stop in the distance that you can see is clear.

Watch the 'Limit Point' as you approach a bend, and you'll notice that it may move. If it becomes closer than your ability to stop in the distance you can see to be clear, slow down and match your speed with the distance to the 'Limit Point'.

'Limit Point of vision' – the furthest point that you can see clearly through a bend or obstacle

Once in the bend and having applied positive steering to negotiate the curve, if the 'Limit Point' moves away from you, it means the road is opening up and you may be able to increase your speed.

On the other hand, if it moves towards you, this means the bend is tightening and you may need to slow down.

This 'Limit Point of Vision' technique means matching your speed to the distance the 'Limit Point' is away, accelerating or slowing down accordingly.

Using this method ensures the right choice of speed and thus the correct gear selection. This will enable you to manage your machine's speed throughout any turning or curve. Your machine will then be on the correct side of the road and you will be able to stop in the distance you can see to be clear.

"If the 'Limit Point' moves towards you, the bend is tightening and you may need to slow down"

How to be a better rider

HOW TO CORNER USING IPSGA

 You must be able to stop in the distance you can see to be clear throughout the bend.

⑤ ④ ③ ② ①

"Match your speed to the distance the 'Limit Point' is away from you."

① You're 80 metres from the bend in the road and the 'Limit Point' of Vision (LPOV) is getting closer than the distance you can safely stop in. Slow down.

② You're 40 metres from the bend. You've slowed down to an appropriate speed and the LPOV is static relative to you. Maintain your speed.

③ You're now 20 metres from the bend. The LPOV is still static relative to you. You're at the correct speed to negotiate the bend. Hold your speed.

④ You're in the bend now. The LPOV is starting to move away from you and the bend is opening up. You can consider accelerating at this point.

⑤ Exiting the bend, the LPOV moves away from you. If there are no immediate hazards, accelerate as the road opens out and plan for the next bend.

 Remember you should apply the 'Limit Point' of Vision technique to junctions and hill crests as well as bends. The same rules apply to all hazards.

HANDLE ANY BEND WITH CONFIDENCE USING THIS CORNERING TECHNIQUE...

Always observe as far ahead as possible, ensuring that the road is clear. Use the 'Limit Point of Vision' technique to maximise your observation and to manage your speed on approaching the hazard.

On a rural road this is the point where the two verges or hedges appear to meet. Correct use of this technique ensures you always enter a bend at the right speed.

1) On approaching any corner, check in your mirrors to see if a vehicle is approaching fast from behind and planning a possible overtake.

2) Position your machine correctly on the road.

Move to the left-hand side of your carriageway on right-hand bends (but mind drains, verges or other nearside hazards).

Move out towards the centre of the road on left-handers

(but take into account any oncoming traffic).

This repositioning increases your view ('Limit Point of Vision') through the bend and makes for smoother steering and progress.

Never position your machine so far over that it could unnerve another road user.

3) Manage your speed so that you can take the corner safely yet progressively. Aim to complete any braking that may be necessary in a straight line and remember your speed must allow you to stop within the distance you can see to be clear in relation to the 'Limit Point of Vision'.

4) Look out for potholes and drains, or anything that could affect your cornering line. Continually reassess your 'Limit Point of Vision' and adjust your speed if necessary.

5) Select the correct gear to maintain a smooth and consistent ride through the corner (avoid changing gear mid-corner). Do it after you have finished braking and before you begin to turn in.

6) Use the 'Positive Steering' technique (see page 38) to lean the machine into the corner with a progressive movement, not a jerky motion. Smooth steering keeps the motorcycle stable and balanced, helping you to maintain your speed right through the bend.

7) As you turn in and your machine settles, apply a balanced throttle – just enough to keep your speed steady, but not enough to accelerate.

8) As the road appears to open and you are able to straighten up, accelerate progressively bearing in mind the riding conditions.

CORNERING FORCES

Almost all crashes on corners are as a result of inattentive, careless or dangerous riding. Other factors, such as worn tyres or slippery road surfaces, are sometimes catalysts, but usually the rider is to blame due to poor observation, poor planning or too high an entry speed into the bend.

Taking a left-hand bend too fast could easily result in you crossing the centre-line straight into oncoming traffic, while a tighter than expected right-hander might well see you on the verge, in a ditch or, worse still, colliding with a tree.

Even minor changes in road surfaces can have a dramatic effect on the handling and stability of your machine, especially at speed or when cornering. Camber of the road surface (a deliberate sloping of the road to aid drainage) can assist you on left-hand bends, but works against you on right-handers. Always observe the road surface you are on, adapting your speed and position accordingly.

> "Taking a left-hander too fast could easily result in you crossing the centre-line straight into oncoming traffic."

BRAKING IN A CORNER

Always aim to complete your braking before you begin to turn into a bend.

This, 'slow-in-fast-out' technique, is the smoothest, safest and often the most progressive way to ride.

Late braking into bends is often used by racers to defend their position in a race, but often results in them exiting the bend significantly more slowly.

Late-braking in a bend can upset your stability, causing you to run wide or lose all control.

Where acceleration sense can't be applied, use your brakes briefly and smoothly between bends.

Where there is no straight 'braking zone' between bends, look for a brief opportunity where you are upright between left-hand and right-hand lean, then use your brakes without unbalancing your machine.

Good observation should mean that you never have to brake 'late', once you're in a bend. However, if you are forced to brake in such a hazardous situation, do it smoothly and progressively.

RIDER CHECKLIST
- Always negotiate corners at a speed that allows you to stop within the distance you can see is clear ('Limit Point of Vision').
- Complete any braking and gear changes before turning into a corner.
- If traffic and road conditions allow, and your speed warrants it, always position your machine for the best view through the corner.
- Avoid sudden braking or harsh acceleration in bends.

EXAMINER CHECKLIST
- Does the rider consider road surface conditions when selecting their speed and line through a corner?
- Is the right choice of speed made?
- Is the correct gear selected to match the speed?
- Does the machine remain balanced throughout the bend?
- Is the machine positioned correctly on the road throughout the entire cornering manoeuvre?
- Is steering smooth and progressive?

Overtaking

A rider has many advantages over a driver when it comes to overtaking: improved view, good power-to-weight ratio and an overall smaller size. As a result, a well timed, well executed overtake is both satisfying and safe

PREPARATION

Firstly, ask yourself whether any overtake you are about to attempt is justified.

Where an overtake is justified, you should make the manoeuvre as safely, decisively and quickly as legally possible.

Before beginning the manoeuvre, assess whether the vehicle may be turning off soon (a post van, milk lorry or tractor) and whether the overtake might be easier a little further on, where the road might widen or straighten.

If you're overtaking a vehicle with poor rear visibility, make sure the driver knows your intentions. Briefly sounding your horn may help. This is particularly advisable when passing distracted drivers, lorries, caravans or tractors and trailers, as these slower-moving vehicles are able to turn very quickly, often without any signalling or braking.

THREE-STAGE OVERTAKING

Police riders are taught a three-stage method of overtaking. Below you can see exactly how it works in three easy steps.

Combine this technique with good observation, anticipation and machine control, for a fast, efficient and safe overtake every time.

1) THE FOLLOWING POSITION
The following position is a position that allows you plenty of time to react should the driver in front brake suddenly. (see the two-second rule on page 95).

Adopt this position if you have no intention of overtaking, cannot do so imminently due to other hazards, or when prevented from doing so by solid white lines or no overtaking signs. In the absence of any other hazards, and if it is safe to do so, you can move directly to (3), the overtaking stage.

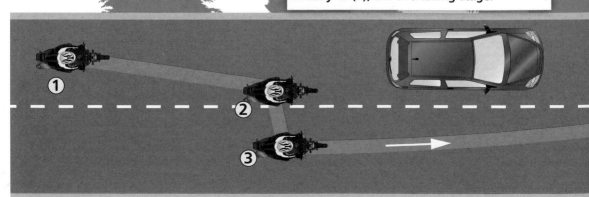

WHEN TO OVERTAKE

Every overtake requires planning, quick thinking and decisiveness. Ask yourself these questions before you attempt any overtaking manoeuvre:
- Is there sufficient clear road to carry out the overtake safely? Is anyone ahead slowing down or turning right?
- Which gear will provide the best acceleration to complete the overtake safely?
- Is the vehicle in front hiding another vehicle that may block my attempts to pull in?
- Is there a slow-moving vehicle that could turn quickly?
- Are there any concealed hazards such as obscured lay-bys, side turnings, entrances, buildings or gates?
- Never overtake at or approaching a junction, even one that might look clear. The

Check your mirrors before any overtake manoeuvre and always be aware of blind spots.

vehicle you're passing may just turn without warning or someone might pull out.

When joining a main road, many ordinary drivers only take the time to look right – this is the cause of numerous fatal, high-speed accidents.
- Observe around and underneath any vehicle you're passing to check all is clear in front of it. Often shadows are a good way to judge whether, for

Before you attempt any overtaking manoeuvre – THINK!
- Is there enough space to get by?
- How fast are any oncoming vehicles in the distance travelling?
- Are there any entrances, side turnings or lay-bys?
- Is the vehicle you're about to pass concealing any other vehicles?
- Are they considering an overtake themselves?
- Is somebody about to overtake you?

This extra attention to detail could save your life.

example, another motorcycle is being obscured by a lorry.
- Never make risky overtakes. If in any doubt, stay back.

2) THE OVERTAKING POSITION
If you anticipate an opportunity to overtake, close in on the vehicle in front until you're in the 'overtaking position'. This is normally closer than the 'following position' and towards the centre line, increasing your view ahead.

Match your speed to the vehicle in front and consider taking a lower gear to pass it.

If the overtake doesn't come off, consider dropping back to the 'following position', and then start the whole process again.

3) THE OVERTAKE
When it's clear, move carefully to the other side of the road to increase your view. If the overtake is safe, accelerate quickly past the vehicle. If it's not, drop back in behind safely and smoothly.

The final part of the manoeuvre returns you safely back to your side of the road in as straight a line as possible.

Consider using mirrors and/or a 'Blind Spot Check' to make sure that you do not cut-up the vehicle you have just passed.

COMMON OVERTAKING MISTAKES

Practise your skills to avoid making the following basic overtaking mistakes:

● Poor gear selection limits your acceleration and lengthens the time you are exposed to danger.

Understand your bike's power delivery for fast, safe overtakes.

● Carrying out an overtake only to discover another vehicle blocking your return position, leaving you exposed to danger or forcing you to 'bully' your way back in.

● Failing to notice buildings and their entrances (building lines), junctions, lay-bys or other entrances that may spell danger.

● Failing to consider that another driver might be planning to overtake when attempting to pass two or more vehicles.

● Planning and executing your overtake so poorly that it has to be aborted at a very late and dangerous stage, e.g: while alongside the other vehicle.

● Gambling on what traffic may or may not come around the next bend, or on the speed of approaching vehicles.

Optimism and risk-taking are not part of advanced riding – always consider what the worst case scenario might be.

● Riding too close behind the vehicle you're about to overtake. Riders of low-powered machines are often tempted to do this.

● Waiting too long in the exposed 'overtake position', on the off-chance that an opportunity may arise.

Minimise the time spent in this vulnerable place.

● Forcing other drivers to react to accommodate your poorly-timed overtake.

● Pulling out to overtake without using your mirrors,

only to discover a faster vehicle is already committed to a manoeuvre behind you.

● Taking a run-up to an overtake. Riders of low-powered machines often try this extremely dangerous manoeuvre, which leaves them travelling considerably faster than the vehicle in front and too close to it.

If the vehicle in front brakes, you're in big trouble.

Remember to match the speed of the vehicle you intend overtaking when in the 'overtaking position'.

● Being indecisive over an

overtake that you should be committed to is as dangerous as rushing into an overtake.

When overtaking, act positively and quickly with good observation, anticipation and control.

● Following another vehicle into an overtake. What if they don't pass as quickly as you think or have misjudged the overtake altogether?

Using other vehicles as shields is dangerous and severely limits your view. What if they suddenly pull in, leaving you to face an oncoming lorry with nowhere to go?

WET WEATHER OVERTAKING

Overtaking in bad weather is more dangerous as visibility can be seriously reduced by spray, and braking distances are significantly increased.

Also remember that, just because you can't see headlights, doesn't mean that there's no vehicle there. Many motorists forget to put their headlights on except when driving at night.

"In a potentially dangerous situation, try to accommodate the driver who's at risk"

Remember that foreign truck drivers will be sitting on the left-hand side of the cab, and that there's a greater chance that they will not see you in their mirrors. Take extra care when overtaking them.

MAKE OVERTAKING EASIER FOR OTHERS

It can be tempting to challenge a dangerous or poorly-planned overtake in order to teach the other driver a lesson. Rise above this behaviour and make life as easy as possible for the overtaker. You want them as far away from you as possible.

● If you are not intending to overtake, consider leaving a generous gap in front of you for overtaking vehicles to pull into. Otherwise they may have to attempt a doubly-dangerous two-vehicle overtake.

● Use your mirrors carefully and regularly.

● Never compete for an overtaking opportunity with another driver or rider.

● If a potentially dangerous situation develops during an overtake manoeuvre, attempt to safely accommodate the overtaking driver by accelerating or braking to provide them with a big enough safety gap to pull into. If you don't, they may just decide to occupy your space.

How to be a better rider

CROSS-HATCHINGS

Cross-hatchings separate potentially dangerous lanes of traffic. You must know which ones can and which ones can't be ridden on.

Crosshatchings bound by a solid white line are usually found separating carriageways on the approach to a motorway slip road.

They should not be ridden on except in an emergency or if the police direct you to.

Cross-hatched areas surrounded by a broken white line are used to separate traffic on some roads that may have had three lanes. You may enter these areas where you can see it is safe to do so, but beware

of debris that may lurk there.

These 'hatchings' usually appear on roads with high accident rates. Take care when overtaking not to surprise other drivers who are not expecting anyone to be riding in this cross-hatched zone.

Refer to the Highway Code for more detail.

The solid lines surrounding these chevrons cannot be crossed except in an emergency

TWO-WAY ROADS WITH THREE LANES

Britain's dangerous three-lane roads have been much improved with the addition of cross-hatchings and solid white lines. Solid double white lines keep drivers going in one direction to two lanes and those in the other direction to one lane. They should not be crossed, though there are exceptions to this rule. (See the Highway Code).

On some roads, particularly on hills, a solid white line is paired with a broken white one. This normally gives the

uphill traffic two lanes (so that slow traffic has a 'crawler' lane) and faster downhill traffic just one. However, where the broken white lines are on the side of the single lane, traffic in this lane can cross the line for an overtake if it is safe to do so.

While the markings are clearly

defined, you should always take care and observe intently on three-lane roads, as other drivers may not have your appreciation of the system.

Keep an eye on the people carrier. If you're in its blind-spot, it might inadvertently pull out in front of you.

OVERTAKING AND DUAL CARRIAGEWAYS

Dual carriageways are among Britain's most demanding roads, because, while the speed limit is the same as a motorway (70mph), there are many more potential hazards to deal with. For example:
• Bicycles, mopeds and tractors are allowed to use dual-carriageways.
• Usually there is no hard shoulder for broken down vehicles to pull over onto.
• Side turnings may not have slip-roads. Slow traffic emerges straight onto the carriageway
• Vehicles can emerge from lay-bys at low-speeds.
• Traffic can join or leave the carriageway through gaps in the central reservation.
• Pedestrians are allowed to cross the carriageways.
• Drivers in the right-hand lane may slow down to turn right across the central reservation.
• Learner drivers can drive at 70mph on dual carriageways.

"Dual carriageways are among the UK's most demanding roads, with many unique hazards."

RIDER CHECKLIST
• Always try to help others to overtake as safely as possible.
• Think about whether you really need to make an overtake.
• Apply the correct overtaking method defined in the 'three-stage overtaking' guide.
• Always plan for the worst.
• Make sure building lines are spotted early and approached with caution.
• Dual carriageways present many more hazards than motorways.

EXAMINER CHECKLIST
• Are overtakes carried out smoothly, safely and decisively?
• Is the machine correctly positioned throughout?
• Does the rider match their speed to that of the vehicle they intend overtaking when in the 'overtaking position'?
• Are mirrors, signals and gears used correctly?
• Are building lines spotted early and approached with caution?

Riding in town

The extra demands of urban riding require significantly enhanced observation and anticipation. This section helps you perfect this essential aspect of your motorcycling

THE EXTRA DEMANDS OF TOWN RIDING

Denser traffic and more pedestrians make town and city riding far more intense than riding on the open road.

Hazards are also more likely to be concealed and there are more junctions and traffic lights etc to deal with. The only way to cope safely with all these potential dangers is to observe and concentrate intensely, spotting them and taking the appropriate measures to be prepared for them as early as possible.

Local knowledge is useful in town, but should never lure you into a false sense of security as most accidents occur near home, where road-users are most complacent.

Where advantageous, position your machine for the best view ahead, commensurate with safety, using the information gained to ensure you're in the correct lane as early as possible.

ROUTE OBSERVATION IN TOWN

Good observation in town helps you to spot many hazards and identify plenty of useful riding information.

Here are some important things to look out for:

● Parked cars can obscure hazards. As you pass them, choose a speed and road position that gives you enough reaction time if, for example, a door is opened without warning or someone steps out.

● Spot tell-tale signs that a vehicle is about to pull out: angled wheels, exhaust smoke and illuminated tail-lights etc.

● Look out for pedestrians who are using traffic crossings incorrectly. Many start crossing when the green man 'beeps' without even looking to see if any traffic is approaching.

Also keep an eye out for 'late runners', who make a dash for it as your lights turn green

● Be aware of pedestrians near schools and pubs at key times, and near offices and stations etc at all times.

● Allow cyclists plenty of room as you pass them. Look for

Cars, cabs and crossings. It's a jungle out there!

them at junctions and allow them space for a 'wobble'.

● Watch buses and other tall vehicles up ahead. They can give an early warning as to traffic movements.

● Lorries and buses can obscure important road signs. Looking ahead for signs will minimise this problem.

● Delivery vans often park in awkward places, so take extra

care when passing them.

Look underneath them to spot the feet of pedestrians who may step out into the road unexpectedly.

● In some cities, taxis may make unexpected manoeuvres (u-turns, sudden stops) when they spot a fare. Be especially prepared for this when riding near places like railway stations and shopping centres.

FILTERING

One of the biggest advantages of biking, especially in bigger cities, is the opportunity to filter through congested traffic. Indeed many riders are attracted to biking for this reason alone, only to find how much fun biking is generally.

A comparatively high view-point, together with a good power-to-weight ratio, narrow width and short length give riders many advantages when it comes to congested situations.

Be aware though, some road-users believe that filtering through traffic is illegal and can react to it in a hostile or obstructive manner.

In fact, the Highway Code acknowledges that motorcyclists can filter in traffic and advises that this should be carried out safely and slowly.

If done incorrectly, filtering can be a very dangerous practice. So what is good practice when it comes to riding through heavy traffic? There are three key points to bear in mind:

● The speed of the traffic through which you'll filter.

● The speed differential between your machine and the traffic around you.

● The amount of space available to you.

FILTERING SPEEDS

Filtering in traffic flowing at speeds above 15-20mph should be avoided, as vehicles at this speed can change direction with little or no warning.

Also, the speed differential shouldn't be more than 10–15mph above that of the slower-moving traffic, to allow you sufficient time to react to any hazards. The more distance between you and slower moving vehicles, the greater the speed differential can be.

Good machine control is essential to safe filtering – your concentration needs to be focused mainly on traffic in the near and middle-distance.

Look for overtaking 'stepping stones' when you want to pass a queue of slower-moving traffic. Observe to ensure that the gaps are big enough to accommodate your motorcycle before committing to the move

OBSERVATION AND 'STEPPING STONES'

As well as observing the near and middle-distance when filtering, the advanced rider makes use of peripheral vision. This is an effective way of spotting minor changes in the traffic around you.

Look well ahead to plan your route, and use your peripheral vision to monitor traffic on either side of you. If you see something moving unexpectedly in your peripheral vision, scan around to check it out. Once satisfied, return to the distance vision and repeat.

Avoid target fixation – when your vision fixates on one particular thing, such as a vehicle in the foreground – as any escape route becomes invisible to you. Advanced riders observe, scan, identify, predict, prioritise and act.

In lines of traffic, use distance vision to identify safe 'landing points', that you can move to one at a time, just like stepping stones across a stream.

Always be aware that any gaps could be filled by drivers without warning. If a driver sees a fleeting opportunity to move into a faster lane don't assume they will be checking their mirror before they do so.

COMMON ERRORS WHEN FILTERING

When filtering past traffic, think about the following questions:
- Do you have an escape route planned at all times?
- Have you allowed sufficient distance from other traffic to give you time to react?
- When passing a high-sided vehicle, could a pedestrian step out from behind it?

- Where vehicles start moving off, if one remains stationary are they letting someone or something out?
- When a driver is left space to emerge from a side turning and turn right, will he be looking left as the bonnet of his car extends beyond the line of traffic. Is he likely to spot a filtering motorcyclist? (See the picture below)
- Look into vehicle mirrors, can you see the driver?
- Are they looking at you? If not, they probably cannot see you, and will not know that you are there.
- Advanced stop lines exist in some towns and cities for cyclists – motorcycles should stop before them, not in them.
- If you don't need to be close to the vehicles you are filtering past – move well clear. You are easier to see if you are separated from them, and have more room for manoeuvre if one of them changes direction.
- Approaching traffic lights – if there is a long vehicle stopped at the stop line – can you get to the front of it before the lights change? If not – don't start the overtake (especially not down the nearside of an articulated truck indicating left).

At first glance, this looks like a good opportunity to filter...

... but the advanced motorcyclist will have noticed the gap in the queue and the break in the chevrons, and anticipated the unsighted car emerging

How to be a better rider

STATIONARY TRAFFIC

One very dangerous aspect of urban riding is to filter between the kerb and stationary traffic, as it is not uncommon for drivers or passengers in a jam to open their doors unexpectedly.

Passengers cannot make use of the rear-view mirrors as they are angled for the driver, and few will ask the driver if it is safe to open the door.

If you look closely at a car door, the top edge has the appearance of a blade – not something that you want to be hitting at any speed!

Finally, along the kerbside you will also have to deal with drain covers, protruding kerb stones, leaves, litter and, possibly, wet road markings.

ROAD SURFACES IN TOWN

Urban roads can be more slippery than country roads as the coating of oil and rubber on the streets becomes more polished by the constant traffic.

Take care in dry weather, but remember that a light shower (especially on a hot day) is likely to make road surfaces particularly hazardous.

Oil on the road in places where vehicles stop regularly, such as at junctions, unfortunately reduce grip where it's needed most.

High friction compounds (like Shell-Grip) are applied to road surfaces near hazards (roundabouts, junctions and traffic lights etc) and accident black spots. Moving from these high-grip compounds to normal Tarmac can unbalance your machine, particularly in the wet, on bends and when leaning heavily.

Finally, slippery spilled diesel is common on roundabouts and bends near petrol stations, due to vehicles being over-fuelled.

High-friction compounds like Shell-Grip are common near hazards and accident black-spots

Road surfaces change frequently in town. You'll also have drains, manhole covers, speedbumps, surface repairs and potholes to deal with

BUS LANES

Many cities now allow motorcyclists to use bus lanes.

Riders may be authorised to use them, but drivers who cross these lanes will be looking out for a bus or coach, not a motorcycle or scooter.

Beware at junctions for vehicles turning into or out of them. Plan your filtering well but consider every vehicle passed as an overtake in its own right. Be especially considerate towards cyclists.

Above all, give yourself time to react by maximising the distance between you and other traffic and by keeping your speed, relative to the other traffic, down.

"When stopping in traffic always aim to "Face a Space"

This is one reason motorcycles are suited to city traffic

SLOW-SPEED MACHINE CONTROL

Slow-speed manoeuvring is an essential part of the CBT (Compulsory Basic Training) test, yet few 'experienced' riders can do it properly.

The prevailing belief is that practising manoeuvring with a larger machine should not be encouraged in case the rider drops it. Surprisingly, the opposite is actually true.

Mistakes on a lightweight bike can easily be corrected, but, as the size of the bike increases, the need for practise is even more important.

Riders who can't control large machines at slow speed, will struggle in dense traffic or at awkward junctions, and end up devoting most of their concentration to machine control rather than on the traffic around them.

It's far better to practise this essential skill in the comparative safety of a controlled area with expert assistance. Once you have mastered control of your machine at low speed, you will be free to concentrate fully on other traffic hazards.

Most IAM Groups offer training days to help riders develop their manoeuvring skills. IAM examiners also check that you can control your machine at slow speed.

CONFIDENCE IN CONGESTED CONDITIONS

City riders, used to congested conditions, are generally more assertive than those who ride predominantly on quiet country roads. A city rider may appear pushy as they make progress, but their style is suited to their congested surroundings. It helps avoid jams, and, assuming they know what they are doing and where they are going, their decisive manner shouldn't cause any problems.

Adapt your riding to suit the situation around you. Be as decisive and assertive as conditions require, always aim to make good progress and give yourself room to manoeuvre, by carefully positioning your machine.

This is especially true when stopping behind stationary vehicles in a queue. Always position yourself so that you can easily manoeuvre past the vehicle in front if it stalls or fails to move away.

In addition this enables you to move out of the way if the vehicle behind is having difficulty stopping in time.

Imagine a triangle on the ground with the base along the rear bumper of the car in front and the point towards you (see below). Aim to avoid entering the triangle. In that way you'll never become 'trapped'.

Stay back from the stationary vehicle infront...

...and you'll always have a clear escape route if you need it

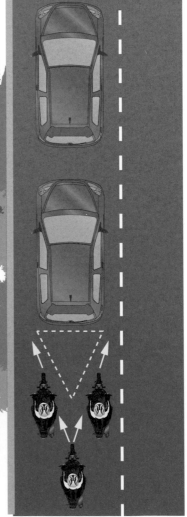

STOPPING ON HILLS

Don't hold your machine on the clutch when you stop on a hill as it causes overheating and premature wear. Cover the rear brake, this is the bike's equivalent of a car's handbrake.

When stopping on a hill in traffic, always leave extra space in front to allow for the vehicle in front rolling backwards.

RIDER CHECKLIST
● Riding in town requires highly-developed, selective observation skills to process all the information you'll have to take in.
● Always pull up so that you are not in the triangular area immediately to the rear of the vehicle ahead.
● Practise your manoeuvring skills until they become instinctive, so that you are free to concentrate on the traffic situation around you.
● Good anticipation is needed to spot unexpected movements by cyclists, parked vehicles and pedestrians.

EXAMINER CHECKLIST
● Does the rider observe all adverse road surface conditions and position accordingly?
● Are signals, road markings and road signs observed, obeyed and approached correctly?
● Does the rider avoid blocking other vehicles and causing an obstruction?
● Is the machine correctly positioned on the road at all times?
● Is the rider confident and courteous?
● Are slow-speed manoeuvres performed competently?
● Is the rider able to filter effectively when conditions allow?

Riding in the countryside

Smooth, sweeping rural roads take some beating when it comes to fun. Use the following techniques to develop safe and smooth country riding

OBSERVATION ON THE OPEN ROAD

Riding on country roads requires an entirely different set of skills to riding in congested towns.

Rural roads are arguably the best place to exploit your abilities and get the most enjoyment out of your riding.

Traffic is usually light, you can make use of your comparatively high vantage point (and better observation skills) to look over hedges and across bends to safely maintain a higher average speed. Finally, the roads are more interesting and you'll need to make well-judged overtakes.

The same level of planning and concentration is required, but you'll be dealing with an entirely different set of hazards and sources of information.

Use all the selective observation skills you have developed, but also consider:

● Taking extra care in case people or vehicles suddenly appear around isolated houses, especially on 60mph roads.
● Looking well ahead (over the hedges, where possible) to spot oncoming traffic in the distance, especially trucks, tractors or low sports cars, often not visible above hedge lines. Also look for potential overtaking zones and plan your

The line of hedges, trees or telegraph poles often, though not always, denotes the direction the road may take around the next bend. Use this information to your advantage when planning ahead.

arrival time to coincide with a gap in the oncoming traffic.
● Drains that were once at the side of the road may gradually move further into the road due to erosion of the verges. Hitting these at speed is likely to destabilise your bike.
● Livestock in the fields might indicate that there is mud on the road, especially if they are cows that need milking daily. You should also be prepared to encounter a flock of sheep around every bend.
● On fast country roads, even something as simple as a side turning or gateway to a field can become a potential hazard.

When you spot one, consider repositioning your machine on the road to give you more time to react, reducing your speed and covering the brake, then, if a vehicle does appear, observe to see if they have noticed you. Try to spot side turnings early and take extra care when approaching buildings.
● Holes in hedges are often found on particularly sharp or tightening bends, and are usually created by some unfortunate rider or driver who has overshot the corner and gone straight on. Treat them as a reminder to take care and to keep control of your speed.

Moving out (safely) towards the centre
of the road, allows you to take a
smoother line through bends

How to be a better rider

The section of road you can see is clear and dry. But what lies around the bend? Be prepared to deal with the worst

Caution! While distracted by the cars on the right, don't miss the concealed exit on the left

ROAD SURFACES

Rural road surfaces can hold any number of surprises for the unobservant and unwary rider.

Always be ready to encounter a hazard around the next bend and be prepared to alter your speed and line accordingly. Always be prepared for…

- loose gravel
- mud
- wet leaves
- potholes
- raised or sunken drains
- dead animals
- deep puddles
- extreme cambers
- smooth and slippery patches of road surface
- tightening bends
- fallen branches
- debris from farm machinery

Loose road surfaces are common after winter. They can be lethal to motorcyclists. Take care

Roadkill presents a danger to motorcyclists

Hitting a puddle like this on a motorcycle could easily result in a total loss of control

On a bend, even a small amount of mud like this spells danger to bikers

SAFE STOPPING DISTANCES

On a smooth, satisfying, traffic-free rural ride, it's easy for even an experienced rider to go too fast.

Always apply this rule: can you stop within the distance that you can see to be clear on your own side of the road?

Always be prepared for the worst, whether that's horse riders, cyclists, oncoming vehicles overtaking a slow-moving tractor, a broken down vehicle or even a farmer with a herd of cows.

Remain a safe stopping distance behind other vehicles and allow extra braking time if someone is driving too close behind you.

If you find yourself following a large van or lorry, drop back a little to gain a better view around them.

On single-track roads, allow double braking distances, as

any oncoming vehicle needs as much space to stop as you do.

RIDER CHECKLIST
- Practise early observation and riding techniques relevant to rural areas.
- Pay attention to the road surface you're riding on.
- Identify hazardous side turnings early and prepare for them.
- Hone your selective observation skills.
- Always be prepared to stop in the distance that you can see to be clear and on your own side of the road.

EXAMINER CHECKLIST
- Is there evidence of good observation and lateral scanning skills at all times?
- Are all signals, road-markings and signs spotted, obeyed and approached correctly?
- Does the rider observe the road surface, looking out for hazardous conditions?
- Are building lines spotted early and approached with due caution?
- Is the rider's judgement of speed and distance competent when overtaking?
- Is good progress made, taking account of road, traffic and weather conditions?
- Is proper restraint shown in the right places?

Motorway technique

JOINING A MOTORWAY

When joining a motorway from a slip road, use your offside mirror to help match your speed to that of the traffic in the left-hand lane of the motorway. Where appropriate, give a right indicator signal, allowing drivers on the main carriageway time to react to your signal and pull into the middle lane.

Plan your acceleration on the slip road so that you don't have to brake or accelerate further to join the traffic flow.

Constantly use your mirrors to check the main carriageway and other traffic around you, and never commit to changing lanes without considering a 'Blind Spot Check'.

If you cross over the motorway on a bridge before joining it, take the opportunity to check out the traffic flow below. It allows you to spot severe hold-ups, giving you the chance to take another route.

On the motorway, ride in the left lane until you have adapted to the speed and traffic flow around you.

> ⚠️ **It is dangerous to run out of fuel on a motorway. Do not join a motorway if you think you may not have enough fuel to reach the next petrol station. Stopping on a motorway hard-shoulder is extremely hazardous, and riding at 50mph in the slow lane to eke out your last few drops of fuel can be just as risky.**

DIFFICULT APPROACHES

Joining a motorway isn't always straightforward.
● When a slip road rises up to join the main carriageway, your vision and anticipation may be limited, meaning you'll have less time to judge the traffic flow before merging.
● To minimise this problem, avoid racing up the slip road and stay well back from the vehicle in front by applying the two-second rule (Page 95).
● On short slip roads you have to be decisive. That may mean you need to accelerate firmly to achieve a safe merging speed.
● Some slip roads have cross-hatchings to separate the lanes of traffic. Those bounded by a solid white line can only be entered in an emergency.
● Look ahead and plan your approach early. Select the lane that lets you merge most smoothly. The right-hand lane is usually the best choice, but you may occasionally want to use the left lane as it merges further along the motorway.

LEAVING A MOTORWAY

Motorway junction signs are usually positioned a mile and half-a-mile in advance. Use them to plan your exit speed and lane position early.

Junction countdown signs appear 300, 200 and 100 yards before each exit. Judge your exit speed carefully, especially after riding for long periods at high motorway speeds.

Lift your vision to see further ahead and make sure you are never caught out by a short or sharply-curving exit slip road.

Beware of diesel spills on exit slip roads.

Use your mirrors and consider a 'Blind-Spot Check' as you leave the motorway, especially if you take the right-hand lane on a multi-lane exit slip road.

Check your fuel level, and consider checking the traffic-flow on the carriageway before joining a motorway

RIDER CHECKLIST
- Observe traffic conditions carefully as you approach a motorway.
- Use you mirrors regularly.
- Consider a 'Blind Spot Check' when changing lanes.
- Match your speed to the traffic flow in the left-hand lane when joining a motorway.
- Maintain good lane discipline.
- Watch your speed when leaving a motorway and particularly if the slip road is short or bends sharply.
- Plan your exit from the motorway in good time.
- Watch out for diesel on entry and exit slip roads with sharp bends.

EXAMINER CHECKLIST
- Is proper use made of mirrors and 'Blind Spot Check' where appropriate?
- Is an understanding of positioning and traffic flow displayed?
- Is good judgement displayed when joining a motorway?
- Is acceleration sense used on the slip road, to join with traffic in the left-hand lane?
- Is the left-hand lane used in plenty of time when exiting a motorway?

Note: not all test routes will feature motorway evaluation.

On the motorway

Make good, safe progress on all Britain's motorways with these simple advanced-riding skills.
Here we tell you how to stay stress-free and smooth on our fastest roads in any traffic conditions

CONCENTRATION AND OBSERVATION

Riding on motorways can become monotonous and you need to concentrate hard to stay alert and observant.

Yes, motorways can be boring. You don't have to accelerate, change gear or brake much, the view is often unchanging and there's relatively little steering input needed. It's easy for your mind to wander in these conditions.

Treat motorway riding like a high-stakes game of chess.

Plan a route, anticipate traffic movement and be ultra-observant, constantly checking speeds and distances all around your machine. Do all this while riding smoothly, safely and progressively.

LANE DISCIPLINE

Select the correct lane for your speed and planned route and constantly observe the movements of vehicles around you, including regular checking of your mirrors.

Stay in the left-hand lane when possible, but avoid diving in and out of it constantly.

Drivers on UK motorways often display poor lane discipline. This causes frustration and problems for other drivers. It can even lead to crashes.

You'll often find traffic gravitates into the right-hand lane to avoid inconsiderate

drivers who remain in the middle lane when not actually intending to overtake.

Never be tempted to teach them a lesson. Do not flash your lights or sound the horn. Simply overtake them as safely and as soon as you can.

SPEED

Riding faster than the 70mph speed limit on UK motorways is illegal.

Always aim to travel at an appropriate speed for the road conditions. However, it's easy for your speed to creep up on a modern machine, so check your speedometer regularly.

Statistically, motorways are the UK's safest roads, but they are still the scene of numerous incidents and many are policed by speed regulation devices designed to maintain safety.

SLIP ROAD COURTESY

As you approach and pass an entrance slip road leading to your carriageway, observe the flow of traffic on it, and consider whether you should move into a right-hand lane to help the vehicles merge and to avoid being impeded yourself.

Lorry drivers will be particularly appreciative of your courtesy, as they are less able to vary their speed to match the traffic flow. If they are forced to slow right down they become a mobile motorway hazard.

KEEPING YOUR DISTANCE

At 70mph on a dry motorway, it takes an alert rider over 21 metres to react to a hazard, and at least 75 metres more to stop. That's at least 96 metres between spotting a hazard and stopping your machine.

This demonstrates just how dangerous it is when some drivers or riders follow other vehicles at a distance of just four or five metres, or less!

Keeping a safe distance increases your view around the vehicle ahead giving you extra thinking and braking time.

Use the two-second rule – stay at least two seconds behind the vehicle in front.

Better still, if you're happy with your cruising speed, stay 100 metres behind the vehicle in front. This distance is easy to judge as the white motorway marker posts are positioned 100 metres apart.

Consider where in the lane to position your machine. Can you see your lane's road surface in the distance? If you cannot, then consider positioning your machine so that it is offset from the wheels of the vehicle in front, or slightly further offset so that you can see the road surface ahead.

Debris from vehicles often ends up in the centre of the lane. It lies there, waiting to be struck by any motorcyclist who's following a car too closely and in the middle of the lane. In this position, they can't see the road surface ahead and what lies on it.

TAILGATING

Tailgating is an increasingly common problem on Britain's roads. Avoid getting wound-up by this dangerous driving style – instead let tailgaters pass as soon as they can.

If a persistent tailgater is proving a distraction, don't be intimidated, simply look to move out of the way quickly. Consider slowing down and moving into the left-hand lane to encourage them to pass.

Many drivers, following a rider positioned on the nearside of their lane, inadvertently judge their following distance from the car in front of the motorcycle, rather than the motorcycle itself. This means they end up travelling far too close to the bike. In this case, consider repositioning your machine to the offside of the lane. You are then directly in the line of sight of the following driver. If this makes no difference, consider moving over to let the driver past.

On busy motorways it can seem impossible to maintain a safe (two second) following-distance. Leave a space that big and inconsiderate drivers will instantly fill it. Some may even undertake you and pull-in in front. Despite this, always aim to keep a safe following distance behind other vehicles.

Try to brake in a way that doesn't surprise the vehicle behind you. Often, that driver won't be adhering to the two-second rule. To protect yourself, aim to spot hazards early, thereby extending your braking distance and giving the following driver time to react.

In urgent situations, consider using the space between lines of traffic, not only to further extend your braking distance, but to avoid becoming the 'meat in the sandwich' if the driver behind doesn't react in time and hits the car in front.

How to be a better rider

CHANGING LANES AND OVERTAKING

Use your mirrors and 'Blind Spot Checks' with care when overtaking on a motorway.

When required, signal early, giving other road users time to react – many will happily accommodate your manoeuvre. Change lanes gradually and never expect or force other drivers to get out of your way.

Acceleration may sometimes be necessary, but avoid getting in the way of faster vehicles.

In heavy traffic, use the signal as a request, before you plan to change lanes. It is a matter of courtesy and allows following drivers time to accommodate your intended manoeuvre.

Finally, adjust your speed so that it matches the traffic flow in a faster or slower lane. Don't compromise your safe following distance (or that of the vehicle behind you) when changing lanes, and always look out for vehicles aiming to pull into the same space as you from another lane.

Your indicator signals should only be used to inform others of what you intend to do, not to order them to get out of the way. Watch out for drivers who try to dictate to other road users by leaving their indicators on for prolonged periods.

Ride courteously and in a planned way. Where safe, accommodate other drivers by changing lanes to allow them in or by slowing/accelerating to create a safe gap. Only use your signals when someone will benefit from the information, and always consider a 'Blind Spot Check' before making your manoeuvre.

In congested traffic, if your lane is moving faster, you may pass traffic on your right.

Consider filtering (see page 81) when traffic speeds drop below 10–15mph, but don't use this as an excuse for blatant 'undertaking', and avoid lane hopping.

Beware when traffic is static. It is not uncommon for occupants to open their car doors to get something from the boot or to get out to see what's causing the holdup.

COMBAT FATIGUE

Motorways are fast, safe but often boring places to ride. The monotony of covering long distances, with very little riding input can lead to complacency and fatigue. To counter this:
- Consider taking an alternative, more interesting route, perhaps on an A or B road. Check your map for parallel routes or set your Sat Nav to avoid motorways.
- Ensure you have the very best waterproof and windproof clothing you can afford. The wind-chill factor at sustained high speeds, especially in the wet, drains concentration over long periods.
- Every time you stop for fuel, make sure you drink a bottle of water. This will help keep you hydrated and improve your levels of concentration.
- Consider a hot drink in cold conditions.
- Avoid heavy meals, they make you sleepy. Instead eat fruit or salads while you're on the road. You can always enjoy a more substantial meal when you arrive safely at your destination.
- Wear ear plugs. These

will protect your hearing, minimising fatigue and making it easier for you to concentrate on riding well.

MOTORWAY WARNING SIGNALS

Motorway roadside and gantry warning signs are there to advise you of dangers ahead, speed limits and carriageway closures, even if a problem isn't immediately obvious.

Make sure you are familiar with all the signs in the Highway Code.

Matrix signs give detailed information and are often used on busy motorways to impose temporary speed limits during rush hours. This slows traffic to keep it flowing, avoiding the dangerous stop/starting seen on many UK motorways.

Gantry signs displaying speeds in a red circle are mandatory and are often enforced with police safety cameras.

Think 'safety' when broken down. High-visibility jackets can be good for your health!

THE MOTORWAY HARD SHOULDER

Motorway breakdowns can usually be avoided if you take good care of your machine – especially your tyres, oil, coolant and fuel levels.

The hard shoulder is an extremely hazardous place to be. To minimise the danger, pull over to the far left side, put your hazard warning lights on if you have them, then get yourself and your pillion onto the verge behind the barrier (and to the rear of your machine to avoid flying debris if a passing vehicle strikes it).

Stay near your machine or find the nearest emergency phone (the direction of which is marked by arrows on a marker post and is never more than half-a-mile away).

On rejoining the motorway, use the hard shoulder as an acceleration lane to match your speed to the traffic flow. Avoid any debris (delaminated tyre tread or exhausts) in your path.

> "The nearest emergency phone on a motorway is marked on a post, and never more than half-a-mile away."

RIDER CHECKLIST
- Position your machine safely behind the vehicle in front, using the two-second rule.
- 70mph is the limit, not a target speed.
- Practise lane discipline.
- Do not let your riding skills or concentration lapse on long, boring journeys.
- Use good observation, anticipation and courtesy to merge smoothly when changing lanes.

EXAMINER CHECKLIST
- Are speed limits observed?
- Is a safe following distance maintained?
- Is the use of mirrors, 'Blind Spot Checks', signalling and lane discipline of a high standard?
- Are speed, distance and other traffic movements judged competently?

Riding on motorways in bad weather

Britain's notorious weather can cause major problems on any road, and our busy motorways are no exception

RIDING IN HEAVY RAIN

Motorway spray, caused by heavy rain, can cut visibility to virtually zero. Lorries throw up an almost impenetrable wall of water that can coat your visor and wipe out your view for vital seconds.

Plan wet-weather motorway overtakes carefully. Hang further back out of the spray and observe the road and traffic ahead. When conditions are most suitable (the route ahead is clear and straight), move safely, quickly and decisively past the lorry. With good planning your view

should be impeded for only a fraction of a second at worst.

Heavy rain creates pools of water across the carriageway that can cause a bike to aquaplane. This is where the tyre skims across the water and loses contact with the road surface totally.

Aquaplaning affects your control by reducing the effect of steering and braking inputs. If you see water pooling or streaming across the road, do not brake or accelerate, instead ease off the throttle, grip the handlebars firmly and try to

steer straight ahead. Standing water will tend to pull on the handlebars and you may need to make corrective inputs when your front tyre regains full contact with the road surface.

On hills, diagonal streams of water often cascade across the carriageway. Be extra vigilant and slow down gradually in very wet conditions.

Braking distances multiply in the rain. Compensate by slowing down, looking further ahead and increasing your following distance – especially if there is diesel on the road.

FOG

- Avoid riding in fog altogether if it is possible.
- Many people travel far too fast and much too close together in foggy conditions.
- As always, ensure you can

stop safely within the distance you can see to be clear ahead.
- Constantly ask yourself, if the next thing you saw in front of you was a stationary vehicle involved in an accident, would

you be able to stop in time?
- Keep to the left-hand or centre lane.
- Ride on dipped headlights.
- Don't take any chances. Riding in fog is risky enough!

STRONG WINDS

- Strong cross-winds and turbulence can severely unsettle your machine and even blow you off course.
- Be prepared for strong, unsettling winds when you ride on to a flyover or viaduct with no protective embankments.

Riding past HGVs at speed has a similar effect.
- Be aware of the effects of strong winds on other vehicles

like high-sided lorries, vans and caravans. Give them a wide berth, plan your overtake away from the high-risk locations mentioned previously and consider leaving the middle lane as a 'buffer zone'.
- Machines with a lot of bodywork tend to be more affected by side winds than unfaired machines.

ICE AND SNOW

- Avoid riding in extremely wintry conditions. Is any journey really worth the risk?
- Only in the most extreme weather are motorways affected by settling snow.

Usually snow ploughs and gritter lorries keep them clear. However, slip roads and hard shoulders don't always get the same treatment, so take extra care when riding on them.

Also be aware that bridges are particularly susceptible to re-freezing and invisible black ice. The ice on bridges is also often the last to melt.

- In sub-zero conditions, ride at a safe speed, allow greater braking distance and make extra-smooth steering and braking inputs to avoid unsettling your machine.
- In extreme winter conditions, stay in a higher gear and don't make any sudden inputs (throttle, brakes or steering) as these may cause a slide.
- The left-hand lane carries more traffic, so is likely to be the most clear of snow and ice. Stay there as much as possible.
- Do not put your wheels on, or try to ride obliquely through the lines of slush and ice that collect between lanes.

RIDER CHECKLIST
- Do not travel in severe weather conditions unless absolutely essential.
- Slow down, extend your following/stopping distance as conditions deteriorate.
- Don't underestimate the dangers of fog. Get off the motorway if necessary.

EXAMINER CHECKLIST
- Does the rider adapt to bad weather conditions?
- Is speed reduced and stopping distances extended in poor riding conditions?

Riding in tricky conditions

Advanced riders are able to ride with skill and precision in all conditions, including difficult situations in the day or at night. These tips will help you achieve that goal

Speed is more difficult to judge in the dark – especially approach speeds

RIDING AT NIGHT

The fundamental rule of a systematic approach to your riding – that you must be able to stop within the distance you can see to be clear – is especially important when riding at night.

Away from street lighting, your vision will be limited to the range of your headlight, and this varies massively between dipped and full-beam. Therefore, it makes sense that you slow down when you're riding on a dipped headlight. If you find your speed creeping up, remind yourself how dangerous it would be if you suddenly came across another vehicle, a tyre carcass, a pedestrian or even a stray animal in your headlight beam.

If your headlight illuminates 40 metres ahead, you'll have just 1.5 seconds to react and stop at 60mph. Realistically, you'll still be travelling at around 40mph when you hit the obstruction.

On unlit roads, ride on full-beam when possible. Always consider others and don't blind them with your lights.

Remember, your lights can warn others of your presence. Clean them regularly, as road grime quickly reduces their effectiveness and the distance you can see clearly ahead.

THE BENEFITS OF NIGHT RIDING

Riding in the dark isn't all danger and drawbacks.

Empty night-time roads make journeys quicker and less stressful; vehicle headlights give early warning of their presence, and you can even use other vehicles' light beams to work out where the road goes next.

Make use of all the observation clues available to you, the pattern of street lights, reflections of other vehicles lights and where tail lights of other vehicles go ahead of you.

Don't be complacent though, speed is more difficult to judge in the dark – especially the

speeds of approaching vehicles – so you should still take care and adhere to all the daylight riding rules.

The benefit of night riding – quiet roads in the city

Keep your headlights dipped in town. Don't dazzle the driver you're following

DAZZLE

If an approaching vehicle forgets to dip, quickly look to the left side of the road, beyond the headlights to avoid being temporarily blinded.

On a dual carriageway at 70mph you cover 31 metres (about seven vehicle lengths) per second, so even if it takes only five seconds for your vision to clear fully, you will cover a huge amount of ground with temporarily impaired vision.

With practice, this avoidance technique becomes habit. Give the offending driver a brief flash to remind him he's on full beam, but never stay on full-beam yourself to retaliate.

RIDER CHECKLIST
- Be aware that it's more difficult to judge distance and speed in the dark.
- Ensure you can always stop safely within the distance you can clearly see in your headlight beam.
- Maintain and clean all your lights (including numberplate light) regularly.
- Select dipped and main beam with consideration for others and the conditions you're riding in.
- Stop for regular breaks when making long journeys, especially at night.
- Tiredness is a killer. It affects reaction times and concentration.

How to be a better rider

EYESIGHT AND FATIGUE

Many eyesight problems are enhanced when riding at twilight or in the dark.

A dirty or scratched visor impairs a rider's vision. Never use any tinted visor at night.

Riding long distances in the dark is very tiring on the eyes as they have to constantly adjust and work much harder than in the daytime.

Every year, many collisions are caused by drivers falling asleep at the wheel. Don't think that just because riders are out in the breeze they are exempt from this danger.

Whenever possible, avoid making long journeys after a full day at work, have a light snack (not a heavy meal) before setting off and avoid alcohol or drugs. If you start to feel tired whilst riding, find a safe place to stop. Take a break at least every two hours. Once stopped, remove your helmet, have a good stretch and rest your eyes. Drink plenty of fluid as this keeps you hydrated and helps you to concentrate.

Consider taking a quick nap ('power-napping' significantly increases awareness) and only get back on your machine when you feel fully refreshed.

Avoid riding between 12am and 6am when the effects of tiredness are most pronounced.

RIDING IN FOG

Always ride within the limits of what you can see. This is especially important in foggy conditions, as the lack of vision seriously affects your sense of speed and distance.

Do your best to avoid travelling in thick fog as it is one of the most dangerous riding conditions you'll encounter. If you have to ride, only travel at very low speeds. That said, even this can put you at danger from drivers who won't slow down and gamble with their lives and those of other road-users.

Minimise the danger by following these simple rules:-
● If fog develops, slow down and switch on your lights.
● Fog density can change in a few metres. You can go from a light mist to a pea-souper in a second. Ride accordingly.
● Moving traffic helps disperse fog a little. Be careful about overtaking the lead vehicle of a queue – there could be a 'wall' of fog ahead of it.
● The strain of peering through thick fog quickly makes you tired. Take regular breaks.
● Take extreme care as you accelerate in preparation for any overtaking manoeuvre.
● Never go ahead with a manoeuvre based on the fact that you can't see any lights. Not everyone will remember to put their lights on.
● Never be pressured by tailgaters into riding faster than you feel is safe.
● Likewise, don't ride faster than you feel comfortable with, just to keep up with the rear lights of the vehicle in front.
● You are required by law to use your headlight when visibility is reduced to 100 metres or less.
● Avoid using main beam in fog. The bright illumination reflects off the fog, impairing your view by creating a 'wall of white' in front of you.
Use a dipped headlight.
● Fog can suddenly appear in dense patches. It generally occurs first (and is thicker) near water, e.g: on coastal roads and near rivers and lakes.

RIDER CHECKLIST
● Postpone a journey if conditions are very bad.
● Slow down in fog, so that you can stop within the distance you can see is clear ahead.
● For the best visibility in fog use a dipped headlight, not main beam.
● Avoid overtaking or trying to stay in touch with a vehicle that you think is travelling too fast for the conditions.
● Allow enough space in front, so that you can pull up in time if the vehicle in front were to stop dead in a collision.
● Remember fog makes the road damp and covers your visor, both inside and outside, with moisture that can impair your vision further.
● Keep the inside of your visor clean, this delays the build-up of condensation.
● Try having the visor open slightly to create an airflow which reducess misting.
● Consider fitting an anti-fog attachment to your visor.
● Do you ride at an appropriate speed when visibility is reduced?
● Do you ride a safe distance behind vehicles in front of you?

RIDING IN WINTER

Freezing winter weather creates many new hazards for motorcyclists, from poor visibility to a potentially lethal lack of grip.

Try to avoid riding in these difficult conditions if at all possible, but if you have to, you'll need extra concentration, anticipation and the following techniques to negotiate these hazards safely.

RIDING IN LOW TEMPERATURES

- Some machines have a built-in external temperature gauge. Use it as an early-warning system to assess riding conditions. An indicated temperature of three degrees centigrade or below means that slippery conditions are possible.
- Adjust your riding to the constantly changing conditions. Always ride within your own – and your machine's – limits.
- Observe other road users to see how they react to the conditions ahead. Alter your riding style accordingly.
- Stopping distances can increase dramatically in winter. Look further ahead for possible hazards, stay focused and make sure you are far enough behind the vehicle in front to stop comfortably if it brakes.
- Riding long distances in bad weather can be tiring. Poor visibility and the wind-chill effect takes its toll on your concentration. Stop for a break at least every two hours.
- If you are losing the feeling in your hands, stop in a garage or services, get a warm drink and make use of the hot-air

dryers to get feeling back into your hands.
- Make sure you wear suitable warm, waterproof clothing
- Consider some form of heating element, either in your clothing or on your machine. Heated handlebar grips are a great option.
- In slippery conditions make use of the higher gears as it minimises wheelspin.
- If a driver tailgates you in wintry conditions, be prepared to pull over and let them pass.
- In freezing conditions, make an effort to ride as smoothly as possible. Clutch, acceleration and steering movements should be smooth and progressive and braking should be done early and gently.
- If there is salt on the road the surface will be noticeably more slippery. Avoid banking the machine more than is absolutely necessary.
- Bridges are also particularly prone to icing. They freeze first and thaw last.
- The worst freezing usually takes place at night and in the early hours. Avoid riding at

these times if at all possible.
- The grooved finish on concrete road surfaces often collects water, which freezes in winter making them particularly slippery and hazardous.
- Be aware that as ice melts, and other drivers' confidence returns, the conditions can remain extremely hazardous.
- Even after any snow, slush or frost has gone, ice can remain on road surfaces shaded by trees and buildings.

Be aware when crossing shady sections of road that your machine's grip may be significantly reduced, especially on bends.
- Black ice is almost invisible and it reduces a bike's grip to zero. If you hit black ice, there is little you can do to control your machine.
- Always make sure your lights and mirrors are clear of dirt and ice before setting off on a winter journey.
- Beware that your visor doesn't become frozen, either through freezing moisture on the outside or your breath on the inside.

How to be a better rider

RIDING IN SUMMER

Road surfaces become surprisingly slippery in summer, especially after rain or even a heavy dew. Debris particles (dust, rubber, oil etc) can also build up on the road surface, severely reducing grip levels. Tarmac becomes slippery when it gets 'polished' after a long dry spell

Here are some essential riding tips for summer:

- Summer storms can create flash floods. Excess rain water takes the line of least resistance, which often means flowing down or across a road. If this happens, slow down to an appropriate speed, keep a careful eye on the depth of the water and prepare yourself for reduced visibility and grip.
- Try your brakes immediately after riding through large puddles or floods.
- Never ride through deep water at speed. Just 10mm of water can cause a machine to aquaplane, taking control from the rider for vital seconds.

  Deeper water will pull on the handlebars violently. It can cause an instant change of direction or even a fall.
- If you think a puddle or flood might be too deep for your machine to ride through safely, look for evidence of the water depth (relative to verges or kerbstones etc).

- Ride through floods slowly and smoothly in first gear. Keep your revs high and slip the clutch.
- Never enter floods that would immerse your machine's air intake or sparkplugs. Your engine will stop instantly leaving you stranded, and potentially with damage to your engine. (Check the manufacturer's handbook.)
- Don't enter a flood when there is traffic coming in the opposite direction. Their 'bow wave' could cause your engine to become flooded.
- Worn road surfaces are often re-covered with loose stone chippings in summer. Take care not to skid on them, especially where the chippings 'pool' on bends and at the road's edges.

  Also, hang well back from the vehicle ahead to avoid your machine getting pebble-dashed.
- Pick the driest road surface to ride on. Don't position just for vision if it means riding on a wet surface when there is a dry line close by.
- Maintain good visibility by keeping your visor and lights clear. While you may have reasonable vision in the dry, the minute it rains or becomes dark your view may become dangerously limited.

RIDER CHECKLIST
- **Prepare your machine for winter riding every autumn.**
- **Use your controls more smoothly when riding in slippery conditions to avoid skidding.**
- **Read the road ahead to spot slippery patches. Look for shady areas, bridges and places where water might have gathered.**
- **Wear the best clothing (for protection and warmth) you can afford. Make sure your visor is clean and unscratched. Consider heated clothing and/or heated handlebar grips.**
- **Don't get so cold that it affects your concentration. Stop often to warm up.**

EXAMINER CHECKLIST
- **Does the rider adapt to bad weather conditions?**
- **Is speed reduced and are stopping distances extended in poor riding conditions?**
- **Is the road surface observed carefully, especially in bad weather?**
- **Does the machine appear to be well maintained?**
- **Is the machine ridden with restraint and with extra sensitivity when roads are slippery?**
- **Does the rider make use of extended braking distances and display enhanced acceleration sense in slippery conditions?**
- **Are the machine's mirrors and lights clean?**

Roadworks and breakdowns

From motorways to C-roads, UK highways are plagued with roadworks. Here's how to handle them efficiently and safely

ROADWORKS AND CONTRAFLOWS

A sophisticated system of warning signs and coning keeps traffic as safe and mobile as possible through roadworks and contraflows. Special care needs to be taken when negotiating these hazards.

• Change lanes in good time, using excellent observation and clear signalling. Forcing your way in just before the carriageway narrows causes a chain of braking that can make traffic further back come to a complete standstill.

• 'Zip' merging – where each vehicle let's one other vehicle in – is a more effective way of keeping the traffic moving.

• Aim to stay in the left-hand side of your carriageway in contraflows. Changing carriageways and riding next to oncoming motorway traffic in narrow lanes, separated only by a line of plastic cones, increases the risk of a collision.

• Keep an eye out for debris like exhaust pipes and tyre carcasses on the carriageway, especially in the centre of lanes where car tyres rarely go.

• Consider filtering to the front of a queue at temporary traffic signals where there is sufficient width to do so, and you have identified a bike-sized space between the lead vehicle and the 'wait here' sign. If you do, thank the driver for leaving

you that space, even if it was unintended. It lessens the likelihood of competition when the lights do eventually change.

First aid, emergencies and personal safety

Most riders will encounter or be involved in a collision at some point in their riding careers. How they react can sometimes mean the difference between life and death

ACCIDENTS

Avoid becoming an 'accidental pedestrian' vulnerable to danger, when you get off your machine at the roadside. Consider all the dangers posed by passing traffic and act accordingly. In the event of an accident:

1) Ensure that everyone involved is out of immediate danger and consider protecting the crash site from further accidents. Ask another driver if you can borrow their warning triangle (unless on a motorway) and encourage everyone involved to use their hazard-warning lights.

2) Don't park your machine where it may be a hazard to other traffic or where it blocks emergency vehicle access.

In the dark, as the first vehicle arrives, encourage the driver to park so that their headlights illuminate the accident scene.

3) Call 999 (112 on a mobile phone) for help. Give your precise location, and tell them: how many casualties there are; how serious any injuries are; how many (and what kind of) vehicles are involved in the crash and if there are any fuel or chemical spillages.

4) The first minutes after an accident are crucial to the well-being of any casualties.

Do whatever you can to help, even if it is just offering those involved some moral support.

5) Do not move any incapacitated casualties, or the vehicle they are in, unless there is an imminent risk of fire.

6) Switch off the engines of all vehicles involved and apply their handbrakes if possible.

7) Make sure nobody in the vicinity smokes.

8) Approaching vehicles need as much warning as possible of the accident and its location.

Arrange for someone to walk back up the side of the road for at least 100 metres, facing the oncoming traffic flow and giving a clear 'slow down' signal and pointing to where the accident is. If you have high-visibility clothing, consider doing this yourself.

Do not stand in the road.

9) Allocate someone to direct vehicles around the accident. Make sure they are clearly visible by positioning them in the headlamp beam of a stationary vehicle.

REMOVING AN INJURED MOTORCYCLIST'S HELMET

In consultation with various expert bodies, the IAM has created these guidelines for helmet removal.

● If the rider is breathing and there is no danger of choking, leave the helmet on.
● If the rider is unconscious and has stopped breathing, you have less than four minutes to act to prevent brain

damage or death. Here's how to remove a full-face helmet:
● Unfasten the chinstrap.
● It takes two people to remove a helmet safely. One supports the head and neck, the other lifts the helmet.
● Lift the helmet backwards off the chin first then away from the base of the skull.
● Support the head and neck until a surgical collar is fitted.

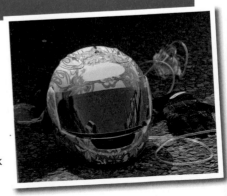

HELPING CASUALTIES

- Only move casualties if they are in immediate danger, as it could aggravate their injuries, causing paralysis or even death.
- Ensure they are breathing. Remove any food or chewing gum from their mouth, loosen their collar (and tie) and undo any helmet straps, leaving the helmet on.
- If you can't detect breathing, consider mouth-to-mouth resuscitation (even if this means removing the helmet – see page 106).

To do this, place the casualty on their back. Hold their neck so that their head falls back, opening the airway. Pinch their nose and hold their mouth open. Cover their mouth with yours and blow firmly to inflate the lungs. Then release the mouth and nose. Check for breathing. If it is not apparent, repeat the procedure until the casualty starts to breathe.

- If the casualty is unconscious, place them in the recovery position, on their side with an arm and leg positioned to keep them there. Turn their head so that it is facing slightly downwards to prevent choking.
- If the casualty is bleeding, apply firm pressure to the wound. If you have a first-aid kit, bandage a sterile dressing firmly over the wound.

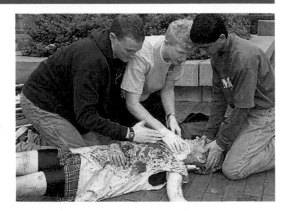

- Prevent fracture injuries from being moved.
- If the casualty is conscious, sitting up in the vehicle and in no immediate danger – do not move them. Simply support their head in case they pass out.
- Keep all casualties warm, especially those in shock. Do not give them alcohol, drugs, food, drinks or cigarettes, as these may aggravate any internal injuries.
- This is basic first aid advice. For more details log on to: www.redcross.org.uk.

How to be a better rider

TRAVELLING ALONE

Let people know where you are going and when you're hoping to arrive. Take a mobile phone.

If you breakdown, and are a woman travelling alone, let the recovery services and Highways Agency know, as you should receive priority treatment. Program emergency numbers into your mobile phone.

If you suspect a following vehicle is anything more than just an inconsiderate driver, ride to the nearest police station or public place before stopping.

WHAT TO DO IN THE EVENT OF AN ACCIDENT

- Never ride away from the scene of any accident without speaking to the other people involved or leaving your contact details.

Always remove the ignition keys from your bike, even if you leave it for just a moment.

- At any accident, give your name, address, registration and, where there are injuries, insurance company details to the other parties involved.

It is your responsibility to get the same details from other drivers or riders involved.

- Uninsured and unregistered drivers are common on the UK's roads. If you're suspicious that the other driver is not driving legally, contact the police straight away.

If they don't want you to call the police, have a look at their tax disc. If this is out of date, other essentials like MOT and insurance may be too.

- 'At fault' drivers often want to pay for repairs themselves, rather than affect their no-claims bonus. If this is the case, take their name and address and check some proof of ID, before they leave.

- Get details of any witnesses. Do this quickly, as they often disappear once everything is under control.

- You do not have to involve the police, but it is best to do so if anyone is injured or there are allegations of dangerous or illegal driving or riding.

If you call for an ambulance or the fire brigade, the police should arrive automatically.

- Even if you only tap or scrape another vehicle in a car park, you are required by law to leave your contact details.

- In a serious accident, don't move any vehicles until the police arrive. If you have a camera phone, take pictures and/or video of the scene, as this evidence is useful in court.

Take notes and measurements if the information might be useful for the police or your insurance company.

- Insurers advise you not to admit liability at the scene of the accident.

- Do not get angry if you are crashed into. Stay calm, swap details quickly, then clear the road to prevent delays.

- If you witness a hit and run incident, write down as many details as possible: vehicle make, model and registration etc. Don't forget though, the victim always takes priority.

- Don't 'rubberneck' when passing the scene of an accident. This invariably causes delays and can even lead to other collisions.

FIRST AID KITS

If you have space in a top-box or pannier, carrying a first aid kit could save a life one day. They're available from stores like Halford's or Boots. Ensure your kit is up-to-date and contains: plasters, surgical dressings, bandages, slings, safety pins, scissors and a knife.

Never offer a casualty any type of medication or drug, as you may leave yourself open to being sued if anything should go wrong.

Another useful precaution is to input an ICE (In Case of Emergency) number into your mobile phone. Emergency services use this to quickly contact next of kin in the event of an accident.

RIDER CHECKLIST
- At the scene of an accident, act quickly and decisively.
- Carry a first aid kit and know how to use it.
- Use your camera phone to take pictures or to record video evidence at the scene.
- In minor accidents where no-one is injured, swap details (name, contact, insurance and vehicle information).
- Do not admit liability and clear the road as quickly as possible.

Thank you

The authors and the IAM would like to thank the following expert riders for their assistance in the photography for this book.
Trevor Ambrose
Claire Beckett
Crispin d'Albertanson
Andrew (Wookie) Longshaw
Meg Morris
David Whitrow

We would also like to thank BMW, Triumph, Norton Way Honda and Tippets of Surbiton for the loan of their motorcycles for the shoot and Arai, Hein Gericke and Frank Thomas who supplied all the clothing and safety gear used.

OTHER IAM PRODUCTS AND SERVICES

Driving Abroad
An excellent 224-page paperback guide written by Robert Davies.
  Ideal for anyone planning to ride or drive overseas.

Riding Assessment
Maintain your advanced riding skills with regular assessments.

Special Assessment
Take your riding to new heights with this excellent high-level riding check-up.

Learn to be an Observer
Become an IAM volunteer and help others perfect their riding techniques. Doing so will help you to improve yours too.

Senior Observer
Take your riding and observation skills to the very highest level and see how good you really could become.

For further information visit www.iam.org.uk

How to be a better rider

www.iam.org.uk

After passing the advanced riding test

After passing the test you should always aim to ride in a way that sets an excellent example to other motorists. What's the point in raising your skills, and then not emphasising the point every time you ride? Having passed the test, you now have the skills to ride safely and progressively at all times, but you should aim to never stop learning and always seek to improve your riding further. As an IAM member you can continue to enjoy further challenges by taking a Riding Assessment or a more stringent test, known as the Special Assessment. The IAM is always looking for new volunteers and observers to help deliver its national advanced riding agenda. Consider retaking your test every few years to keep your riding skills honed to perfection.

Help others to become advanced riders
9 out of 10 riders will tell you that they are above average, yet this is, of course, a mathematical impossibility. However, if you really want to be as skilful as you can, the way forward is to maintain your already high riding standards and consider helping others to do so by joining the IAM group network as an observer.

HOW TO BE A BETTER RIDER - THE ESSENTIAL GUIDE
This essential IAM guide has been written to support the IAM's Skill For Life advanced riding scheme – the world's finest advanced riding scheme for everyday motorcyclists. It contains all the information you need to take and pass Skill For Life. As a qualified advanced rider you are far less likely to crash than a normal rider, so, as well as possibly saving your life, you can also save money on your motorcycle insurance every year.

Skill For Life is facilitated by the IAM
SAFELY • COURTEOUSLY • PROGRESSIVELY

IAM Contact Details
IAM, IAM House, 510 Chiswick High Road, London. W4 5RG

Tel: 0208 996 9600
E-Mail: enquiries@iam.org.uk
Web: www.iam.org.uk
